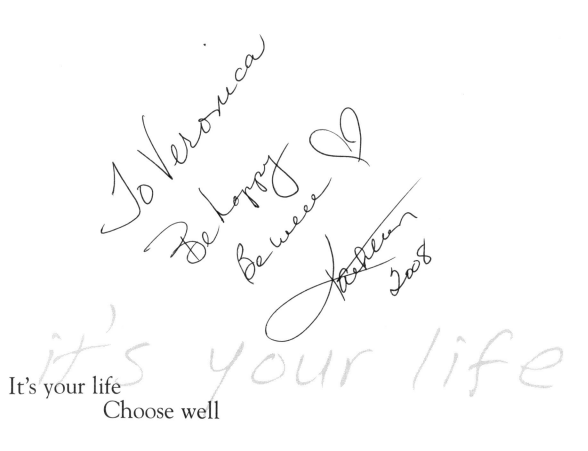

To Veronica
Be happy ♡
Be well
Kathleen
2008

It's your life
Choose well

Dear Reader,

This book is NOT one of those syrupy, touchy-feely tomes in which the author, a self-serving goody two-shoes, shares her *Top Ten Secrets on Perkiness*, her *Fanny-Flatteners Even Great-Grandma Can Do From Her Wheelchair*, or her nauseating innermost thoughts on how a cup of prune juice, if taken daily by each person on the planet, would move us directly to world peace.

This book IS about simple choices you can make to help you be healthier, happier, calmer, saner, and much more balanced. Did you catch that? *Simple* choices. When you add them together, they have a huge impact on your well-being. And not only are they uncomplicated, they're *pleasurable*! That's why they are easy to incorporate into your everyday life.

You're probably skeptical. It's understandable. You've been led to believe that good health requires sacrifice, pain, and an unnatural amount of willpower. You've suffered through high-impact aerobics, tried to figure out what to do with tofu, and own at least a dozen self-help books with titles like *Mind Over Blubber*. Hey, we've all been there.

This book is filled with ideas designed to help you take stock of the choices you make regarding your overall well-being. Decide if they are helping or hurting you. The topics are divided into six sections: physical health, mental health, emotional health, social health, vocational health, and spiritual health. Just read whatever strikes a chord that day, and decide how you can take advantage of the information to improve the quality of your life. You might want to share this book with someone else whose quality of life could use a little boost.

Just remember—*It's Your Life. Choose Well!*

Kathleen Keller Passanisi

It's your

Kathleen Keller Passanisi, PT, CSP, CPAE

First Edition

Thoughts on living a happier, healthier

life
Choose well

Lake Saint Louis   MOVERE PUBLISHING   Missouri

saner life now—not someday

IT'S YOUR LIFE—CHOOSE WELL

Thoughts on Living a Happier, Healthier, Saner Life Now—Not Someday

Kathleen Keller Passanisi, PT, CSP, CPAE

MOVERE
PUBLISHING

Published by:

Movere Publishing

Lake Saint Louis, MO

1-866-MOVERE1

First Edition publication date January 2004
Second Printing March, 2004
Third Printing March, 2005
Fourth Printing March, 2007
Fifth Printing March, 2008
Printed in the United States of America

ISBN 0-9744280-0-0
1. Self help.   2. Gift   3. Health

Cover illustration and design by Steven Michels-Boyce

Book interior and illustration by Trese Gloriod

Creative Contributors

I am grateful to have the opportunity to collaborate with these very creative, talented people.

Bobbi Linkemer & Peter Passanisi	Development Editors
Annie Passanisi	Content Editor
Michael S. McConnell	Copy Editor
Steven Michels-Boyce	Cover Illustrations and Design
Trese Gloriod	Interior Illustrations and Design
Mary Janet Ruff	Right Arm/Left Brain

Dedication

For the most incredible mother,

MaryAnne Donovan Keller,

who loved books almost as much as she loved me.

contents

Contents

First Things First · 16

23

physical health

mental health

emotional
health

designed to provide a little insight into conscious choices we could make to improve our personal well-being. The information was timely, easy to digest, and almost always involved something that was pleasurable to experience. Three nights a week you could hear me sharing these thoughts, which I delivered in an almost meditative style. (I know that's hard to believe if you've ever heard me in person.) Honestly, I was so smooth and sounded so mellow that I'm surprised people listening on their car radios didn't nod off at the wheel.

I loved doing radio—and not just because it suited my wardrobe. It was challenging to say something useful, understandable, and worthwhile in 90 seconds. It kept me learning and growing, and my own well-being improved because of it. Plus, it was gratifying to be involved in something so positive. The show got great feedback.

My radio work ended when the station was sold. I filed away the columns I had written and gave them little thought until my husband suggested I do something with them. When I showed my collection to a few respected writer pals, their response was universal: "Make these into a book. You've done so much work. Why not provide this information to all those who've asked you for it over the years?"

Gee, when they put it that way, how could I not? So, here it is, folks. The information has been revised, updated, expanded, and—at long last—completed.

How Are You Supposed to Use this Book?

Frankly, you can use it any way you like. However, I designed the material so that you can skip around, read a page a day, reflect on its value to you and the choices you have been making, and finally determine if and how you might choose a little more consciously—a little more wisely. You may want to work on one suggestion a week, or even one a month. If the idea grabs you or strikes a chord, really think about it whenever you have a few minutes. (I realize a lack of time is often an excuse for not doing anything for yourself. Do it anyway.) If you really hate what I have proposed, ask yourself why you are feeling put off by the suggestion. Insight is possible either way.

I have divided the book into six dimensions of well-being, which is how I have always taught wellness classes. You can call them mind, body, spirit, whatever you choose. Each idea put forth in a particular section will provide benefits not only in that area of your health, but in all the others as well. Believe me, they are all connected.

I find I get the most from a book when I scribble down my reactions, questions, great insights, and big plans in the margins as I read. I suggest you do the same. I've left you plenty of white space. Go for it. Personalize it. A book sitting on the nightstand in mint condition serves only as a coaster. As you read, I'm confident you will find creative ways to add your own ideas to the mix. I hope you'll share them with me (I'm serious).

So What's the Bottom Line?

As I said before, nothing I'm offering is meant as a substitute for good medical care. All suggestions are intended as preventives to illness or as complements to your formal medical care. For example, a cancer patient receiving chemotherapy might benefit from relaxation and visualization exercises. An elderly person recovering from a broken hip might be aided by using therapeutic touch or humor in conjunction with his physical therapy. For those of you who are generally "okay," the suggestions can't hurt (besides, why settle for being "okay" when you can be great?). Hopefully, my offerings might serve as that ounce of prevention that keeps you from ever needing the pound of cure.

Health is meant to be enjoyed. Maintaining our well-being can and should be a pleasurable experience! Banish the thought that taking care of yourself has to be boring, tasteless, uncomfortable, or otherwise unappealing. Dive into this book and try the suggestions that appeal to you. If they make you feel better (which they will), you will be motivated to continue. It's amazing how activities so simple can be so effective! A happier, healthier, saner life is attainable, but it's up to *you*.

What are you waiting for?

physical

relating to your body

This is usually the easiest to understand of the six dimensions of wellness. It includes all the parts of your body that can be seen and touched—bones, muscles, heart, lungs, kidneys, nerves, brain, blood, skin, eyes, ears, etc. How is your overall physical health? Do you feel energetic, strong, and pain free? Or are you tired, weak, and uncomfortable?

Have you been taking care of your body? Consider the choices you have been making. Are they working for or against you?

in this section

Body Image
Breathing

health

Exercise
Food
Inactivity
Pain
Sleep
Smell
Sunshine
Touch
Visiting the Doctor
Water

body image

Body image. Oh, Brother! Lord knows I've been dwelling on my curves since I saw a bumper sticker the other day that read, No Fat Chicks.

These three words really bugged me because I know how much pain that sentiment causes so many women and girls. American females are compared to a ridiculous ideal body type inhabited by a few high fashion models and movie stars. Face it. They lucked out in the gene pool! Like the golden few, the average female mannequin is 5'10" and no larger than a size 2! Come on now, that is nowhere near the average female body! Trying to be pencil-thin causes us a lot of problems, including an increase in anorexia, bulimia, amenorrhea, and brittle bones, just to name a few. And don't get me started on the damage caused by the emotional burden of feeling unattractive. Here's a really eye-opening piece of news from the National Institutes of Health: of all the risks of being overweight or obese, probably none has a more adverse effect than the psychological suffering of feeling fat.

It all boils down to our society's extreme preoccupation with weight. Millions of women weigh themselves daily. As you read this, the majority of women think they weigh too much and almost half are struggling with some kind of weight-loss program. Are you one of these women? Is your daughter? Even girls as young as eight or nine have begun to obsess about their weight! Somewhere, down deep, we have this feeling that being a little soft or rounded is a sign of self-indulgence and a weak will.

It's time for a wake-up call! The fact is healthy women may have up to thirty percent body fat. It tends to be distributed more in the areas of the breasts, abdomen, hips, and thighs. This is believed to be due to female hormones and the fact that women's bodies are built for bearing children. However, this does not mean that we can scarf down cupcakes and write-off the consequences as nature's plan. The number of obese American women is rising. Most of the time, it can be treated with a healthy, balanced diet and exercise. (This, by the way, is a good idea for almost everyone, regardless of size or gender).

In my book (no pun intended), we need to do some serious thinking about what is promoted as ideal. Shouldn't beauty be redefined as being physically fit and generally healthy? I encourage women to aim for strong, firm muscles that carry them easily through the demands of their lives. I also recommend meals that provide them with high energy and balanced nutrition. It's also incredibly important that you be well informed. Your doctor and/or a few trusted websites can tell you just how much fat you need to lose (or gain) in order to be healthy. That's important. The number on the scale is not the issue. It's the percentage of body fat that counts. If you have lots of muscle, you may believe you are overweight when you aren't. Conversely, your scale may put you in an acceptable weight range, but you have too little muscle and too much body fat. You can buy special scales to calculate the ratio of body fat, or you can check with your health club. Websites also often provide tips and support group information.

Remember, mannequins are not real people. They don't need to eat, nor did they inherit a big bust or wide hips from their parents. Just follow these simple steps, and I'm certain the outcome for most women (and men, for that matter) will be better self-image, stronger self-confidence, and greater overall happiness.

And by the way, if you see that guy with the tacky bumper sticker, let me know where he's hanging out. I'd like to have a little chat with him. Twenty bucks says he's got a beer gut!

body image

reflections

Reflections

breathing

Breathing. It's not the kind of thing you think about too often, unless you're having trouble doing it. Then it becomes your *only* thought. Most of the time, however, it just happens without our conscious intervention. It's obvious that breathing is a bodily wonder we take for granted.

The respiratory system really is a work of art. We come into this world with it humming rhythmically along in fine form, naturally breathing correctly. Watch sleeping babies or young children breathe. Their tummies gently rise and fall as they inhale and exhale.

This pattern of "belly breathing" is the correct way to breathe. It's important for several reasons. "Belly breathing" moves air deep into the lungs, providing us with a better supply of oxygen. The act of deep breathing is also a natural relaxant. That's why we're often advised to "take a deep breath" when we need to calm down. It's a nifty little built-in feature we all have that really, truly works.

Unfortunately, most of us miss out on these advantages as we get older. We're constantly told to "Suck it in," and so we turn to "tummy tamer" pantyhose to conform to cultural standards. What we don't realize is that this renders correct breathing almost impossible. Instead, we wind up using upper back and chest muscles to breathe. If you notice your shoulders rise when you inhale (and they are somewhere up around your earlobes), you are taking shallower breaths and may wind up feeling tense or tired.

It takes conscious effort to change this pattern, but you can retrain yourself to do it right. The payoff is big. Want to give it a try? Come on. Right now. Lie down on your back. (No really, stop reading for a second and lie down. NOW!) Bend your hips and knees, placing your feet flat on the bed. Relax your shoulders, chest, and midsection. Place your hand or a book on the center of your waistline (I've found it works especially well if you use *this* book). Inhale slowly, really concentrating on filling everything from under your collarbones to the bottom of your ribs with air. The hand or book on your tummy should rise. Then exhale slowly through your mouth, as though you were blowing through a straw. Your tummy will fall as you empty your lungs. Repeat this five or ten times. Get up slowly because all that good oxygen might make you a little dizzy.

Practice at night and again in the morning. Then try the same exercise standing up. You have to breathe anyway, so why not do it the way nature intended? Aahhh—isn't that better! Just remember: breathe easy!

exercise

Exercise. Exercise. I've been thinking a lot about it. Unfortunately, thinking is not nearly as effective as actually doing it. If it were, most of us would be in great shape. But the truth remains, exercise is something we *all* need, and it takes effort. It's a vital investment we make in our health. So, where does one start?

First, be sure there aren't any reasons why you should not exercise. If you are over forty or have medical problems, I strongly recommend you talk with your doctor first. If you are in good health, but have not exercised in a while, you probably know what will happen if you don't start slowly. Months of no exercise followed by an evening of shooting hoops with your teenagers equals an inability to bend over and tie your shoes the next day. Not impressive! I know you're probably in a hurry to get results, but it really is important to do this right. So, how do you map out a good exercise program? Let me offer some basic, solid advice.

You need to plan to exercise three to five times a week. (Already you're thinking of fourteen reasons why that's not going to happen. Knock it off.) Not all your sessions need to be long and sweaty to be effective. (Okay, welcome back.)

The first part of your exercise period should always start with a warm-up. Flexibility exercises gently stretch the muscles to increase their blood supply, range of motion, and help to avoid injury. The old bouncing activities, like touching your toes with knees stiffly locked, are out. They can cause more harm than good. Slowly work all your muscles, in all the different ways in which they move. These exercises can be done five times a week for maximum movement with ease. As you stretch, keep moving from one area to the next. This will raise your pulse slightly to get you ready for the next phase of your plan.

The second part of your plan is aerobic. Literally, the word "aerobic" means "living in the presence of oxygen." Physically, it means you are going to get your heart rate up, breathe more heavily, and sweat a bit, too. Walking, jogging, or bike riding are great heart-strengthening aerobic activities. First, you will need to determine what heart rate is best for you to work up to. Clueless? There is a ton of information available in bookstores and on the Internet. When looking for information on the Web, use the words "target heart range" in your search, or check with The American Heart Association for guidelines. If you really don't know what you're doing or haven't exercised since you gave up your hula hoop, you would be wise to join a class to get yourself started on the right foot. Be sure your instructor is certified—not just someone who looks good in tiny short shorts. And forget Jane Fonda's advice, "Go for the burn." That burn is nature's way of telling you to knock it off.

Aerobic exercise needs to be done three times a week at the very least, five times a week for maximum benefit. Do not panic. This can be accomplished with a dance class twice a week, and a thirty-minute walk at a pretty good clip on the other three days. If you want, you can even walk in fifteen-minute chunks (as long as you don't call it a day after one chunk). The great thing about walking is that you can do it almost anywhere, inside on a treadmill, around your block, even in your cubicle at the office. Unless you don't mind a little dizziness, I suggest you march in place. Hint: If you walk at the mall, don't stop to window shop. You also might want to avoid the Cinnabon franchise (and its aroma too).

The third part of the plan is strengthening exercises. Don't start picturing Olympic weight lifters just yet. This is for everyone. The fabulous news is that you can build muscle strength at any age. I repeat, at ANY age. There are lots of studies on the benefits of strengthening exercises for the very elderly.

Strong muscle gets us through the chores of the day. It helps us climb stairs, practice soccer with the kids, and haul our luggage on yet another business trip. It also supports our skeleton and helps keep our bones strong. An increase in muscle tissue is your goal. And the great news is, because muscle burns more calories than fat, being firmer allows you to eat a little more and not gain weight. That's "way cool!"

Good old calisthenics fall into this category. Working with light weights or elastic bands is terrific. Exercises done against gravity, such

as sit-ups or pull-ups, are effective too. With any exercise, start slowly
and work up.

Remember, exercise works if you *do it*. If you are really disciplined and
like exercising alone, that's swell. Otherwise, check out a Pilates class
(great for getting all three parts of the program in) or call the local
YMCA. Hospitals sponsor walking programs and provide professionals
to monitor your heart rate and blood pressure. The list is endless and
the choice is yours!

So that's it—the three components of a good exercise program:
stretching, aerobics, and strengthening. Be sure you choose activities
you enjoy and can do regularly, otherwise the thigh-master, ab-crusher,
bun-buster, and those very expensive cross-country skis will be collect-
ing dust. We all need exercise. Come on, just bite the bullet and do
it. Your body will reward you, and you will love how much better you
look and feel!

food

Food. I know what you're thinking: *If it tastes good, it's either fattening, ultimately fatal, or it's on the Surgeon General's list of toxic time bombs.* Don't even go there because that is definitely not always the case. There's a lot of really great-tasting food that is good for you. Would I lie?

Oh, how I love to eat! Not long ago, I had occasion to dine at a Greek restaurant. The food was fabulous—mouthwatering! Plus, it was healthful: grilled lean meat, fresh vegetables seasoned with herbs, low-fat cheeses, freshly baked whole grain bread, and a little dry red wine to boot. Except for the sugary dessert of baklava (which I just couldn't pass up but split with a friend), the entire meal was nothing I'd kick myself for the next day during Jazzercise. The icing on the cake was the gentleman who served it all so beautifully, saying, "Enjoy. Good health."

You had better believe that I enjoyed every bite. That kind of meal demanded to be savored slowly in courses, with lots of good conversation and laughter. Come to think of it, it's a shame we don't take advantage of food and times like that more often. We always seem to be in such a hurry and will do whatever we can to suit our hectic lives. Where do you think "fast food" came from?

Beware. Most "fast food" can be an express ticket to misery. Many of the offerings are very high in fat and sugar—good for neither the heart nor the hips. We get very little nutrition for all the calories we are taking in. Add that to the fact that we usually eat in noisy, uncomfortable surroundings. If we are really pressed for time, we zip through the drive-up, grab our take-out, and scarf down our cardboard-housed meal while navigating through rush hour traffic. Bummer.

There *is* good news. Many of the "fast food" chains are working to reduce the fat and increase the nutrition in their products. All make available information on the calorie count, number of grams of fat, protein, and carbohydrates in each item. I suggest you find out what you are eating. However, I'm not suggesting that a little of the Colonel's fried chicken once in a while is a mortal sin. Nor do I think that chocolate should be cut out of the diet completely. (In fact, that sounds utterly awful.) Unless you have specific health problems, you can skip a meal or overindulge occasionally and be no worse for having done it. The key is the old tried and true rule, "All things in moderation."

We simply cannot live without food. In this land of abundance, most of us don't have to worry about trying to. If you are lucky enough not to fret about where your next meal is coming from, pay more attention to what it will consist of, and where and when you will eat it. Food is a gift. Learn to slow down and enjoy it. That's the recipe for good health. Bon appetit!

inactivity

Inactivity. It's starting to have much more appeal these days. As I write this, it's dark in the morning when I get up, and it's dark again by five—not to mention cold, rainy, and windy. Yuck. This kind of weather makes me want to pull the blankets back over my head, reset the alarm for spring, and tear up my "to-do" list. In the evening, I want hot comfort food for dinner. To heck with a salad. I crave creamy soups or spaghetti and hot garlic bread. After dinner, I want to sit in front of a warm fire with a good book or turn into a giant couch potato in front of the TV. My old sweat pants and tube socks are becoming the uniform of the days I spend at home. Yep—it's starting to feel like winter.

Unfortunately, humans cannot hibernate like bears do. We need to keep moving all year round. Winter, especially, is the season when a lot of us who walked or exercised faithfully during the spring and summer start to blow it. We don't relish slogging along in the dark, the rain, or the cold, so we give up. Game over. Score? Couch—1 Activity—0.

Don't let this happen this year! Invest in your health and mood. The key is to make exercise convenient and enjoyable. Stationary bikes and treadmills are becoming more affordable all the time and are a great solution for people with schedules that can't accommodate a weekly class commitment or with egos that cannot bear to be surrounded by the bronze, the buff, and the beautiful.

Don't wait until midnight to start your exercise or bury your exercise
bike under a pile of dirty laundry. I tape my favorite show and then
watch it while I ride or walk. It makes the time go quickly and adds up
to an easy thirty minutes or hour. It's also a great way to justify watching *General Hospital* or the latest imbecilic reality TV program (if you
like that kind of stuff).

While you are moving, imagine how fabulous you will look and feel by
next spring if you stick to your exercise routine. You will emerge like a
butterfly from a cocoon. Plus, you will be ready for the beach or that
reunion you were dreading. (Can't you just imagine the look on old
Loretta Lipinski's face? If you're a woman, she'll be jealous that you are
so svelte. If you are a man, she will kick herself for ever having turned
you down for the prom. Ha!)

Don't let excuses like the weather turn you into a slug. You only get
one body, so get off your duff and get moving!

pain

Pain. We don't appreciate it nearly enough. You probably think that sounds crazy, but it's true. We would be in big trouble without it, because pain is the body's way of saying, "HELLO! Something is not quite right." Pain is like a red light on the dashboard warning us that we are about to run out of gas or that we've forgotten to buckle our seat belt. It indicates the need for attention before something more serious happens. The warning light itself is not the problem. It's merely the messenger giving us a "heads up" to a situation that needs correcting.

Like the warning light, pain is just a messenger. It tells you whether you have been making good choices and, subsequently, how you're doing. The aching pain in your lower back may tell you that your baby is getting too big for you to carry. A dull headache may signal the need for glasses or a better night's sleep. The burning pain of indigestion may be warning you that, no matter how good your mama's enchiladas are, the chili peppers are irritating your stomach. Sure, those Prada stilettos you got on sale are fabulous, but your aching feet are letting you know that these are "sit-down shoes," as my mom called them.

We should be grateful that we are able to experience pain. Not everyone can. Often, people who suffer from paralysis or severe diabetes lose their ability to sense pain. Having no feedback system, they are at risk for burns, bedsores, and a host of other problems that can lead to gangrene and amputation.

So, if pain is so vital to keeping us alert, why aren't we more tuned in to it? Perhaps it's because Americans are accustomed to having "pain relievers" readily available. We are bombarded by commercials for products to relieve the pain of headaches, joint pain, muscle strain, indigestion, gas, hemorrhoids—you name it. Our first impulse is to head for the medicine cabinet rather than consider the implication of the pain.

Before you pop that pill, pay attention. Your body's incredible feedback system is trying to tell you something so that you can make the changes that will keep you healthy and reduce pain naturally. Of course, persistent or severe pain is a signal to see your doctor.

Pain really is a neat little feature of the human body. It's not worthless, like spam e-mail. Therefore, before you race to the medicine cabinet in a rush to hit your body's "delete" button, make sure you pay attention to pain's warning. Be grateful that your little messenger is working. After all, a little discomfort now is a lot better than a big problem down the road.

sleep

Sleep. It's in the forefront of my foggy mind right now because I haven't slept in awhile. You know how it is. You've burned the candle at both ends AND the middle. You've underestimated, overcommitted, and are now way past pooped. You realize your "get up and go" got up and went. What were you thinking? You're not Super Person. You know you look lousy in tights (if you just agreed to that statement, I recommend you read the "Exercise" and "Body Image" sections).

And why do we love sleep so? Physically, sleep is a time of delicious rejuvenation, when the immune system is strengthened and vital bodily processes are restored. Mentally, it's a time when we get to be "dead to the world," a pause from life's quick pace. Furthermore, we need sleep to stay healthy. We need even more sleep to recover when we are ill. Most adults require seven to eight hours of sleep every night. Teenagers require even more. Anyone who has lived with teenagers knows that their sleep habits never coincide with other family members or the routine of the daytime world. That's because their biorhythms are different from those of babies and adults. They are naturally more alert at midnight than they are at seven in the morning. Unfortunately, our education systems have not taken that into account when planning the school schedules.

There are blessed times when deep sleep comes easily. We say we were "out like a light," contentedly unaware of the world for a few hours. Unfortunately, there are times when we have difficulty falling asleep, even though we're exhausted. We toss and turn in our beds as our mind reviews the events of our day. It wasn't bad enough the first time. Let's do it again. And again. And again. Worries about tomorrow run like a scary movie on the backs of our eyelids (the lights flicker and the organ moans as the unfinished taxes close in for the kill). Sound familiar?

Temporary loss of sleep is usually caused by excitement, worry, or too much caffeine. More severe fatigue may also be caused by insufficient nutrition, pregnancy, certain medications, and/or a lack of exercise. Insomnia, or the inability to sleep, is a symptom, not a disease. It may indicate a more serious problem like a chemical imbalance, depression, or sleep apnea. These conditions are manageable but require more than nose strips and sprays. A trip to your doctor may be necessary.

Here are a few everyday (or should I say "every night"?) tips for peaceful, rejuvenating slumber. First, create a good environment for sleep. Make sure your bedroom is as comfortable, quiet, and distraction free as possible. Second, avoid alcohol, caffeine, and large meals in the evening. And finally, if you can avoid it, do not go to sleep angry. According to sleep researchers, the best advice is this: Go to bed and get up on a regular schedule and don't try to cram all of your sleep needs into a few extra hours on the weekend. Now, go ahead. Put the book down and crawl up into bed. You've earned a break. Follow this advice and you should be asleep in no time. Sweet dreams!

smell

Smell. The good, the bad, and the stinky. Compared to our other senses such as sight and hearing, most people would consider smell less important. But don't take it for granted!

Our sense of smell has lots of purposes. Smell serves as a protective function, alerting us to dangers like smoke, gas, and spoiled food. Similarly, without a sense of smell, food would be virtually tasteless. We all know that a stuffy nose seems to take the zest right out of food. That's because eighty percent of flavor comes from food fragrances sensed in the back of the nose!

More than sights or sounds, scents command our minds. Once we are exposed to a scent, we rarely forget it. A scent can trigger memories stored long ago. The aroma of bread baking conjures up a clear picture of Grandma working in her kitchen. Burning leaves remind us of touch football games in the old neighborhood. The faint scent of a particular perfume causes a man's heart to beat a little faster as he remembers a past love. Personally, I can't smell suntan lotion without thinking about a trip to Hawaii more than a decade ago. More recently, I sat next to a nice-looking guy on a flight to the West Coast. He was intelligent, friendly, and well-mannered. However, something about him just wasn't sitting right with me. Two hours after we landed, it hit me. He wore the same aftershave lotion as this creepy guy I had one date with in college! Blech! Honestly, the guy on the plane could have been Tom Cruise, and I would have felt the same way. Scent is just as powerful as appearance, if not more so!

Allow your sense of smell to introduce you to a world filled with sensual pleasures. Take full advantage of that nose that is on your face! Pay attention to the aromas that are pleasing to you. Take a few moments to consciously enjoy the scents you like best—perhaps warm chocolate chip cookies, coffee brewing, a new car, roses in the garden, freshly laundered sheets, or your freshly bathed baby.

Add fragrance to your life by wearing your favorite cologne, lighting a scented candle, or using fragranced massage oil. Aromatherapy is more than just a gimmick to sell dead flowers. The sense of smell offers simple pleasures and happy memories at no cost. What a deal! Go ahead. (This time it's okay to inhale.) Aaahhh—that's good!

sunshine

Sunshine. Boy, we all yearned for a perfect sunny day last December when the ice was so thick we wore golf shoes to get to the mailbox. Defrosting the children, we fantasized about a warm, breezy, sunny day. What amazes me is when better weather finally comes hardly anyone goes out to enjoy it. Break and lunchtime are spent indoors while the gorgeous conditions we dreamed of waste away on the other side of the window.

No more! We need to take advantage of sunshine. It's one of those naturally healthy things—taken in the proper dose. Sunshine helps us to metabolize vitamin D for strong bones and teeth. Most high school science students know that. But there is more to it. The sun is also a proven mood elevator. Its light affects the chemistry of the brain, causing lifted spirits and a dandy little natural (and completely legal) high.

A lot of us spend the better part of our waking hours in high-rise office buildings without a view of the outdoors. Shut up in our cubicles, we wonder why we have the blues or our energy seems so low. Hello?

Before you reach for the Prozac, see if a little sunlight
does the trick. Now please do not get me wrong
here, I don't mean lathering the body with baby
oil and basting until golden brown. Remember,
too much is as bad as too little. Incurable skin
cancer is a big price to pay for beauty, don't
you think? Instead, frequent short doses,
with skin protected by sunblock, is good
for body, mind, and spirit.

They don't call it a "sunny disposi-
tion" for nothing! Next time the
blues come to call, get outside
and catch a few rays. Odds are
you will feel better before you can
say, "Pass me my shades!"

touch

Touch. Recently, I was beyond ecstatic when my family gave me what I consider to be the perfect gift. No, not even theater tickets or expensive perfume. They gave me a gift certificate for a one-hour massage by a professional masseuse. The anticipation alone made me relax.

As a physical therapist, I have a deep appreciation for the benefits of touch and massage. I am comfortable with it—as a giver or recipient. I find it sad that so many people rule out the idea of having a massage. They say they would be uncomfortable with a stranger touching them or they argue that it's just an expensive luxury. Some of my more honest friends admit that they would feel embarrassed because they think that they're fat. I remind them that Sven, the gorgeous Swedish masseur, couldn't care less about their cellulite. He is there only for their well-being and pleasure. Could anything be more divine?

Touch is a natural healing tool. We need to be touched! Babies who are not touched develop a condition called "failure to thrive." They are underweight and have below-average IQs. However, studies show that when these babies are rocked and touched early in life, they can gain weight and show significant cognitive improvement.

I don't think we ever outgrow the need to be touched. A good massage slows our heart rate, breathing, and blood pressure. It reduces mental and physical tension and rids us of those little aches and pains. It also provides a time of quiet rejuvenation. However, if a massage just doesn't fit into your budget, all is not lost! Simple acts of touching like handholding and hugs are beneficial, too. And they're free! If you're alone, why not reach for a soft sweater or go let the grass tickle your bare feet. The joys of touch are amazingly powerful and they are all around you!

So, thanks, Family, for not buying me a food processor or a Dustbuster. You've given me something so much better— and I'm touched.

visiting the

Visiting the doctor. A lot of people dread it more than dinner with the boss. Some dread it so much that they simply don't do it. I'm not one of them. Nope. Although I never make a hair appointment or dinner reservation ahead of time, I try to schedule my doctor and dental appointments in advance. And no, that doesn't make me a hypochondriac. It keeps me from worrying about being sick. By visiting the doctor regularly, I'm reassured that I am healthy, and my knowledge about staying that way is up to date. Talk about a load off.

A lot of people put off seeing the doctor because they're afraid of bad news. Bad plan. A delay can cost them their lives. Early detection of cancer, heart disease, diabetes, and high blood pressure saves tens of thousands of lives annually. Others don't go because they don't have a regular doctor or haven't found one they are comfortable with. Let's face it. Talking about foot odor or hemorrhoids is never going to be a blast, no matter whom you are talking to. Get over it. If you don't have a regular doctor, now is the time to get one.

The most important thing is to choose your doctor well. Don't just go on the advice of your mailman, or see a doctor because he happens to your neighbor's second cousin twice removed. What should you look for? First, credentials and reputation. Is he board-certified? Is she respected and recommended by other doctors? Consider affordability. Are your doctor's fees covered by your insurance provider? If you don't have insurance, what are the acceptable methods of payment? Find a doctor you connect with. Can you talk easily about personal matters? Do you feel you can trust him? Are your questions answered to your satisfaction? Are your phone calls returned promptly? What hospitals is she affiliated with, in case you require admission for treatment or surgery?

Finally, look for a doctor who is interested in keeping you well, not just patching you up when you're sick. Think of your doctors as your handpicked team of medical professionals who work together to assist you, advise you, and educate you—and *you* are the captain of the team. Remember, when it comes right down to it, you are in charge of your health, no one else.

Remember the old saying, "An ounce of prevention is worth a pound of cure"? Well, it's true. Do not wait until you're sick. An apple a day may not really keep the doctor away, but a regular annual check-up may save your life.

water

Water. We ache for it on days when the thermometer inches toward 100 degrees and the city issues heat alerts. Dripping with sweat, our dry mouths direct our attention to commercials with icy-looking beverage glasses. Soft drink companies cleverly produce commercials with characters stranded next to a broken down bus in what looks like the Sahara Desert. Just thinking about this type of heat makes you thirsty.

Thirst is good. It's a nifty way the body has of telling us we need more fluid. It's kind of like the gauge on your car that indicates you're a quart low on oil. Interestingly, most of us know that running out of motor oil seriously damages a car, but we're too busy to realize that running out of body fluids can kill us.

The human body is made up of about 60% water. It's everywhere—from inside our eyeballs to the water our brains float in. We're also constantly losing water due to sweating, trips to the potty, and even breathing. Therefore, like our cars, our fluid levels need to be maintained. Just like gasoline, water cannot replace itself. So what can we do?

Although we get some of the water we need from the foods we eat, we need to drink

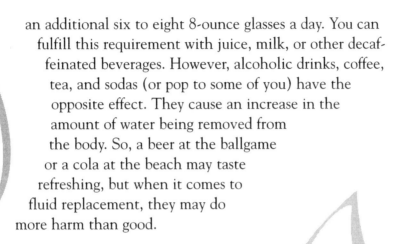

an additional six to eight 8-ounce glasses a day. You can
fulfill this requirement with juice, milk, or other decaf-
feinated beverages. However, alcoholic drinks, coffee,
tea, and sodas (or pop to some of you) have the
opposite effect. They cause an increase in the
amount of water being removed from
the body. So, a beer at the ballgame
or a cola at the beach may taste
refreshing, but when it comes to
fluid replacement, they may do
more harm than good.

Regardless of what most beverage ads claim,
water is the absolute best way to quench your
thirst and keep you hydrated. Unlike any other
drink I can think of, it's the only one that is
difficult to drink too much of. No calories, no
acid, no blackouts. So, drink up. And when you
do, be sure to toast to your good health.

reflections

Reflections

mental h

relating to your mind, intellect, and mental powers

When most people hear the term "mental health," they think of emotions. However, with this model of wellness, mental health refers to the *thinking, knowing* part of the brain. How well does your brain work for you? Are you able to think clearly? Can you learn and retain new information? Do you come up with fresh ideas and creative solutions, or is your thinking foggy? Are you forgetful?

Have you been taking care of your brain? Consider the choices you have been making. Are they working for or against you?

in this section

Age
Change

Goals
Learning
Mistakes
Motivation
Psychosomatics
Reading
The "Shoulds"
Thinking
Words
Worry

Age. A lot of people think about it. More to the point, they worry about it. I heard a great quote attributed to Satchel Paige. He asked someone, "How old would you be if you didn't know how old you was?" What a super question! Hmmm. How would you answer it?

Age is a funny thing. When we're younger, we can hardly wait to be 16 so we can drive. Then, once we get a license, we yearn to be 21—the golden age when we will finally be legal adults and bars will serve us. After that, there are no more ages to look forward to until retirement. We start to dread 30. After that, every five- or ten-year mark is cause for gag gifts of Geritol, black balloons, and those awful yard signs urging passersby to "Honk, Jane is 50 today." Puh-leeze.

I think we do ourselves a major disservice when we think this way. Our brains are programmed by the words we use and the pictures we create in our minds. Try this. Get a mental image of a 90-year-old. Are you envisioning some toothless old geezer or a lean gray-haired adult in jogging shorts crossing a marathon finish line? Sound far-fetched? It's not. Ninety-two-year-old Paul Spangler finished the New York Marathon (and in less time than some of his "twenty-something" peers). I'm willing to bet he doesn't define himself by his age.

I had a great-aunt who used to say, "Honey, you can be twenty-five years old or fifty years young." And then she would tap her temple and say, "It's right here, baby. It's right here." She was right. A great deal of how "old" or "young" we feel has nothing to do with calendar years. Instead, it's based on how well we take care of ourselves in addition to how we choose to see ourselves at every age. I don't intend to be "old" for a long, long time. To quote Cavett Robert, "I intend to die young—at a very old age!"

change

Change. I've been thinking about it a lot lately—not because my daughter has returned from her first month at college with Crayola-red hair, or the fact that the clothes in my closet are almost old enough to be classified as "vintage." No, it's because as I write this, the season is changing. Fall in the Midwest is an undeniable time of transition. The summer's heat and humidity are replaced by crisp, cool air. The green sameness of the leaves becomes a paint box of warm colors. My mom called it "sweater weather"—time to pitch the flip-flops, get out the gym socks, and play a little touch football while you're raking the leaves.

I love the fall, but I have heard more than a few grouches complaining about the change. In fact, they don't like change of any kind; and, boy, do they fight it! They want the same foods week after week. If they eat out, it's at the same restaurant, at the same time of day, on the same night of the week. They vote for the same politicians, watch the same TV re-runs, and hang around with the same crowd of just-like-them people. Any change in their routine throws them for a loop.

Let's face it. We're all going to age, our family structure will expand and shrink, our jobs will never be guaranteed, and the stock market will be as unpredictable as a teenager's mood. Nevertheless, there are those who adamantly resist change. They are fighting a losing battle! Their inflexibility will leave them brittle and breakable.

On the other hand, there are those who flourish in times of change. Thriving on the newness, they are the flexible ones who want the front seat in life's rollercoaster—the first to try sushi, change their hairstyle, and risk quitting a well-paying job to move across the country.

What's the difference between these types of people? In a word, it's "perspective."

The adventurous type sees change as interesting and exciting. The rigid soul finds it frightening and overwhelming. The change-lover winds up invigorated and healthy. The change-hater becomes weak and exhausted . . . Yuck.

It's important to realize that your outlook on change is your choice. Don't fall into the rut of old habits!

If you're having trouble with change, you might want to "meta-think"—which means think about how you're thinking. The best way to change how you *feel* about change is by altering how you *think* about change. You'll feel much better once you do. And isn't that good news, for a change!

goals

Goals.
The last ones you set were probably New Year's resolutions. But, if you're like most people, your plans went by the wayside before the paper hats and champagne bottles hit the trash. Why is that? After all, you really did want to make some changes. What would improve your chances for success? Frankly, it's really not all that complicated.

First, set goals that are reasonable and reachable. It's better to take small steps than a quantum leap. Trying to lose forty pounds by your high school reunion next month is probably unlikely, but ten pounds is doable. Remember—success breeds success. Each time you reach a short-term goal, it increases your self-confidence and resolve. Give yourself small rewards along the way to keep you motivated.

Second, be specific with what you want to accomplish, the time frame it will take to accomplish your goal, and the action plan you will follow. Rather than saying, "I'm going to advance my career this year," say, "I'm going to become eligible for a management position by completing my master's degree, by attending weekend classes over the next two-year period."

Third, write your goals down. Study after study confirms that people who successfully reach their goals almost always committed them to paper and reviewed them often. Don't overdo it. A few goals at a time are plenty.

Finally, conjure up the feelings you will be experiencing once your goal has been reached. How will you feel when you are running your own business, wearing that size ten wedding dress, or flying solo for the first time? This is the ultimate motivation. Dwell on these feelings as often as possible.

Having clear goals has kept hostages alive, built fortunes, and put men on the moon. You probably won't ever be taken hostage, and you may have little interest in going to the moon, but I'm betting that the fortune would not be too tough to take.

Think about it. What would you like to have, do, or be this year? Be specific, write it down, and read it often. Imagine it. Taste it. See it. Feel it. These wonderful feelings of success will keep you on the right track. I'll even give you a practice goal to get you started: finish this book.

learning

Learning. It's not just kid stuff.

I remember getting out of school and thinking that I was finished with learning. Diploma in hand, I assumed I knew pretty much everything I needed to succeed in my chosen field. It took me all of one hour with my first patient to realize that I still had a lot to learn. That lesson has stayed with me.

Learning is a lifelong process. Some of us welcome any opportunity to increase our knowledge or skills. Others avoid learning. Consequently, they become as outdated as eight-track tapes. Hearing so much about layoffs and dwindling retirement accounts makes me wonder about how the people affected are faring. My guess is that those who know how to learn will fare much better than those who never bothered to sharpen their skills. The ill prepared will suffer the highest stress. This stress can wreak havoc, causing everything from alcoholism to ulcers.

Learning new things challenges the mind. It greases our mental wheels and keeps us flexible. The brain needs to be exercised, just as muscles do, to function optimally. There is strong evidence to indicate that people who regularly challenge their minds—through reading, tackling a new project, taking a computer class, etc.—reduce their risk of dementia in later years.

Learning opens the doors to limitless possibilities. If you're stuck in a job that has grown stale, why not explore new outlets for creativity? Expanding your knowledge may be the ticket to a new career. If you have always wanted to study interior design, take up photography, or explore your genealogy, do it! Would you like to get a handle on the latest tax codes, get a real estate license, or be a veterinarian's assistant? What are you waiting for? Check out your local community college's course catalog. If you're not interested in formal classes, join a book discussion club, go over to Home Depot and learn how to wallpaper, or grab a friend and sign up for tango lessons.

It's important to keep your skills fluid and up to date. Regardless of your age or occupation, your brain needs exercise. Learning is a huge part of well-being. It keeps us sharp, youthful, and more in control.

So, turn off the boob tube, hang up the phone, and go challenge your mind! Who knows, you might actually learn something.

mistakes

Mistakes. Golly, have I made some doozies lately! The first involved forgetting to be somewhere I said I would be. This caused me a lot of embarrassment, not to mention a nice chunk of money. The second mistake involved not closing the freezer door tightly, resulting in wasted precious time and some pretty nasty self-talk (not to mention a lot of stinky spoiled food).

My initial reaction to each of these recent boo-boos was fairly typical. Upon first realizing the error, my sense of panic elicited a full-blown stress response—a burst of adrenalin, faster heartbeat, rapid breathing, and a flight of frantic ideas that got me nowhere. As soon as I figured out that the world was not ending, the feelings morphed into frustration and anger at myself for making such stupid mistakes.

But, I have to admit, I'm proud of myself. Although my initial response was common, it was short lived. I caught myself early in the process. I was able to head off an otherwise downward cycle of events by literally stopping and thinking through the situation. You see, feelings are the by-products of thoughts. When your emotions are getting in the way, stop and ask yourself, "What am I thinking that is making me feel _____ (angry, embarrassed, afraid, whatever)?"

Once you get a handle on your thoughts, you will often find that your previous thinking was overblown. In times of stress, our first tendency

is to think globally: "I'll never live this down." "I screw up everything." "Only an idiot would leave a freezer door open." This kind of
thinking gets us into trouble by tearing down our self-worth and
adding to our sense of helplessness. We can avoid this by responding
more specifically: "I don't usually forget things." "I guess it happens to
everyone once in a while." "I must have been distracted by the phone
ringing and didn't realize I . . . ." Whatever.

Cut yourself some slack the next time you goof. We all make mistakes
and the world is not ending. Forgive yourself and let it go. The trick is
to reframe your thinking. Look at it this way: Hey, I have been meaning to give those mystery leftovers the heave-ho, and now it's done!

motivation

Motivation. As much as we *reeeally* want to do something, excuses pop up like roadblocks. "I'm going to quit smoking—just as soon as tax season is over." "I'm going to start exercising—just as soon as it gets warmer." "I'm going to spend more time with my family—just as soon as . . . " Sound familiar?

It's human nature. Our intentions are good, but we're just not in the mood, or we don't have the energy to tackle something difficult just yet. The phrase we often use is, "I have to get *psyched* first," meaning I have to get my head working in the right direction. Mind over matter. But how?

The word "motivate" comes from the root word *movere*, which mean to move, or compel to action. That is exactly what we're trying to do, isn't it? Get moving. Take action. Overcome inertia and get started. Easier said than done? No!

Interestingly, all motivators fall into two categories—pain and pleasure. It's a simple principle to understand. We are driven to avoid discomfort and seek pleasure. Both are very effective, but which do you think would be the better choice? Pleasure, of course. Which one do you think we choose more often? Pain. Sad but true.

When I ask people why they go to work every day, the immediate response is "money." They say, "I have to pay my bills. I need food, clothing, and a roof over my head." Not very exciting, but valid reasons. They are escaping from pain. Show up or be homeless.

Others answer, "I love what I do and the people I work with." They are seeking pleasure. They are driven by the satisfaction they get from their efforts and the enjoyment of relationships they have formed with their coworkers and customers. It's a good bet that they also need the money; it's just not their primary driver. It's not hard to figure out which one will have the easiest time rolling out of bed on Monday mornings.

One of the definitions of the word *motivate* in my laptop dictionary is "to make somebody feel enthusiastic, interested, and committed to something." That sounds a lot better than "to give somebody a reason to do something." Enthusiasm, interest, and commitment are part of the pleasure package and have definite appeal.

How do you take advantage of this? Put the power of imagination and emotion to work for you. Rather than say, "If, I don't lose weight, I'll be buying my clothes from Omar the Tent Maker," envision yourself looking fit and trim. See yourself shopping in your favorite stores, slipping easily into one fabulous outfit after another. Tap into the feelings of that success: you look great in all of them. Your only dilemma is choosing from so many. Taste it, touch it, hear it, smell it in the present tense.

These good pictures and emotions are the drivers that will move you to act and keep you going. Being pulled toward something wonderful is so much better than trying to escape something painful.

Don't waste another minute on the negatives. Pick one thing you really want to work on. Get yourself started and stick with it by concentrating on how great you will feel when you succeed. It works! And that, my friends, is motivating!

motivation

reflections

Reflections

psychosomatic

Psychosomatic. It's a word we usually hear in conjunction with illness. We say, "Your condition is psychosomatic." Not too many years ago, it implied that a problem was "all in your head," meaning it was a figment of your imagination. You may even have been treated as though you were a little nuts.

Medicine has changed a great deal over the last few decades. Psychosomatic illness has become the subject of much research, especially in the areas of stress and how it affects our health.

The word "psychosomatic" comes from two Latin words—*psyche*, meaning "mind," and *soma*, meaning "body." Basically, it means the effect of the mind on the body.

The human body reacts to stressful thoughts in a variety of ways—sweaty palms, shaky voice, nervous stomach, scattered thinking. Headaches, ulcers, fatigue, insomnia, muscular tension, and nausea are often symptoms of stresses such as the loss of a loved one or problems at work. In fact, it's estimated that 75% to 90% of doctor office visits involve stress-related illness. Sounds awful, doesn't it? It's okay, I have good news. It's called "psychosomatic wellness."

Life is all about balance—hot/cold, young/old, yin/yang, comedy/tragedy. In nature, everything has a balance. The mind can affect the body positively just as well as negatively. Rocking a sleeping child in your arms can slow your heart rate and lower your blood pressure. Being in love and feeling loved improves your immune system. Laughter reduces the perception of pain. It's true. My mother could lower her blood pressure by sitting in her favorite chair and immersing herself in a wonderful book. She was a wise woman. I remember calling her to come sit with me when I had the occasional nightmare as a kid. Mom would sit on the edge of my bed, stroke my hair, and counsel me to, "Hold a happy thought." How right she was.

The minds that produce our stress can be used just as well to reduce our stress. All it takes is conscious awareness of what we're thinking and the careful selection of more-positive thoughts. So kick back, think happy thoughts, and let your mind take care of your body.

reading

Reading. There's no doubt about it. If you want to get any-where in life—from a good job, to being able to shop, drive safely, or take care of your family—you must be able to read.

Reading offers more than just being able to understand directions. Reading sparks our imagination. It offers us pleasure and expands our awareness. Sick of the daily grind and its boring routines? Why not travel to exotic lands, solve a murder mystery, or be swept away by romance. All can be done without leaving your easy chair. Talk about a great way to revive our creativity and renew our spirits!

When we read, we challenge our minds. Sir Richard Steele put it best when he said, "Reading is to the mind what exercise is to the body." The brain has to work constantly to understand the words we read, as well as the meaning of events, and emotions being described. Reading stretches our boundaries, exposes us to whole new worlds of information and prevents life's richness from going unnoticed or untapped. You would be hard-pressed to try to find a better example than J.K. Rowling's *Harry Potter* series. Grade-school kids are zipping through her 500-page books and loving every minute of it. Who woulda thunk it?

Too many of us miss out on the pleasures of reading because we're watching TV or have loaded our schedule so heavily we haven't any time for it. If that's the case, change your priorities. With several thou-sand new books published each day, the time has never been better to learn how to read and enjoy it. If you already have a passion for reading, why not volunteer to teach in a literacy program?

The cultural historian Jacques Barzun called reading "the essential stimulus in creating a well-made self—the most fully realized person that you can be." Who wouldn't want that?

I'd continue to tell you about how great reading is but I have the feeling that I'm preaching to the choir. After all, you're reading *this* right now. So just take this as a friendly little reminder. Pat yourself on the back that you have discovered something wonderful. Now turn the page and keep up the good work.

the "shoulds"

The "shoulds." Every day they come upon us like a plague. Things like: "I should be watching my money more carefully." "I should lose a few pounds before summer." "I should spend more time with my kids." "I should be more positive at the office, call my mother more often, eat more green food, work on my taxes, take my cousin out for her birthday, clean under the refrigerator, throw out my raggedy underwear, floss more, rotate the tires on the car . . . " Blah, blah, blah, ad nauseum. You know how it goes.

Complete the following phrase in as many ways as you can: "I really should ____." Give yourself about two or three minutes to jot down everything that comes to mind. My guess is that you will have quite a list. Most of us do. But those little words, "I should" (and their pals "I ought to," "I have to," and "I feel obliged to"), can cause lots of self-inflicted stress. We interpret them to mean "I must" when, in fact, we mean only that it might be "better" if we did something. There's a huge difference.

The "shoulds" are a worse nag than twenty mothers combined—and we bring them upon ourselves! We would feel much more relaxed if we just rephrased things. Then, we wouldn't feel so bad if we didn't do something—and we'd get a bonus of feeling good if we did. Consider it your own personal version of traveling the extra mile or going above and beyond the call of duty. For example, instead of saying, "I *should* lose ten pounds," you might say, "I'd like to lose a

little weight before my daughter's wedding." Which sounds better?
How about this: "I *should* spend more time with my son," versus "I'm
hoping to spend more time with my son." Get the idea?

You might be thinking this is faulty logic, but I promise it's really
not. The real fault is letting our own thoughts ruin our days!
Remember, stress is based on our *perception* of a situation, not the
situation itself. So, give a new way of thinking a try (but because you
want to—not because you "have to," "need to," or "should").

thinking

Thinking. Sometimes, my brain reminds me of an old car I once owned. Even after I had removed the key and was halfway across the parking lot, the engine would still be cachunking along. Of course, my seemingly persistent engine wouldn't always start when I wanted it to. Similarly, why is it that sometimes I can't stop thinking when I would love to be sleeping, and other times solid thoughts come rarely if at all? Is there any hope?

For the most part, the news is good. Although thinking happens naturally and somewhat automatically, it's definitely something we can get a handle on. The trick is a little mind control (no, not brainwashing), a skill that comes with effort and frequent practice.

First, start with slowing down the mind—not always easy in this hectic world. Sit quietly and take a deep breath. Concentrate on the speed of your breathing, gradually slowing it down. It may help to get a mental picture of the thoughts in your mind written as sentences or pictures on a blackboard. Slowly see yourself erasing one at a time until the board is blank. When a thought pops into your head, don't concern yourself with it. Simply acknowledge it and erase it.

Next, work on strengthening the power of the mind. Learn to focus. If a particular problem is plaguing you, write it down. Next, think of three different possible solutions to the problem. Don't panic, they can be stupid or outrageous. Simply create them—don't analyze them yet. Use these three ideas to create three more. This is a type of mental gymnastics that keeps the mind flexible without wearing it out. It's like low-impact aerobics for your brain.

The mind is an incredible, powerful part of the body; but it's only that—one part. Just like your foot can be trained to send a soccer ball soaring, your mind can be taught to work even better. Don't let your mind control you. Learn to control it. Just a thought.

words

Words. "Sticks and stones can break my bones, but words can never harm me." Think again. How do you talk to yourself? Do you say things like, "I'm no good at sports," or "I'm too old for that foolishness"?

Be careful. More and more, we're finding out how much our self-talk affects the way the mind and body function. You see, the brain is a lot like a computer. It can't make decisions on its own. Rather, it reacts to the data or information we feed into it—and the body responds accordingly. It should come as no surprise, then, that we don't always feel so well.

Listen to the way we talk. "You make me sick." "He's driving me crazy." "Oh, I could have just died." "I can't stomach that guy." "What a cross she has to shoulder." "It blew my mind." "Doesn't that just break your heart?" "If he steps on my toes one more time . . ." "That just kills me." "The traffic was murder." "You are a pain in the ___."

We say these things mindlessly, out of habit. And what do we wind up with? Nausea, anxiety, ulcers, sore muscles, corns. At the very worst—death. At the very least—hemorrhoids. It's no wonder. Your brain is just sitting there, waiting for you to tell it what to do. Meanwhile, you respond with enough negativity to make yourself sick.

We need to pay more attention to our self-talk. It's often the basis for who we are today. Not living up to your potential? If you're nervous, timid, or afraid to take a risk, it might be because of the messages you've been giving yourself. "I could never do that. What if I make a mistake? I would absolutely die of embarrassment!" (By the way, I know of no one who has ever actually died of embarrassment). The office grouch whose communication skills attract people like garlic breath probably has not said anything nice to himself since the Nixon administration. On the other hand, confidence, happiness, and health are all great indicators of positive self-talk.

There's no doubt about this. Words are powerful and we have a choice in which ones we use. So, choose words that will keep you well. It's like giving yourself a big hug, without everyone looking at you funny.

worry

Worry. "Worried out of my mind." "Worried sick." Even "worried to death." Clearly, worrying is not a pleasant emotional state. We all know it's not good for us and yet we let it consume us.

Not to worry! There's hope. It's call *cognitive therapy*, or learning to consciously deal with our thoughts. Say that your 16-year-old daughter promised to be back from her date by midnight. It's now 1:00 a.m., and you are "worried sick." Your blood pressure is up, your heart is racing, and your stomach acid is churning. Your mind is creating Technicolor pictures of your daughter being coerced into doing "the nasty" with that weird-looking character she met at the mall (you know, the one with the green hair and the facial piercings?). As you pray for her safe return, you are experiencing all the emotions and negative bodily responses you would feel if the situation was actually happening. But it's not. The door opens and in strolls Kiki, as calm as can be. Upon realizing she is fine, you erupt into an Academy Award–winning parental rage, screaming, "I am going to kill you!" A minute ago you were making deals with God, and now you're going to take her out yourself! Not too rational. You're relieved that she is OK, but you're going to kill her anyway for putting you through that worry. It just doesn't make sense!

The word "worry" comes from the root word meaning "to strangle." That's exactly what worrying does. It chokes off our ability to think clearly. We're just like a car spinning its tires in the mud, expending a lot of energy without any progress.

The next time you are worried, stop. Take a few deep breaths. Think the situation through. What's the worst that could happen? Write down your concerns or talk them through with yourself. This will keep your mind from spinning. Then, make a list of actions other than worrying. Remember, no matter how much you worry, it won't change a thing except your sanity and your health. Alternatives? You could take your mind off your concerns by watching an old movie. You could get a cellular phone so your daughter could call you if the need arises. Or you could ground her for the rest of her natural life. There, isn't that better already?

mental health

reflections

Reflections

reflections

Reflections

emotional

relating to our feelings,
the emotions that move us

Your mood has a tremendous impact on your life. It governs the course of your day. So, how have you been feeling lately? Are you happy, calm, and confident? Or are you frustrated, angry, and fearful? Feelings are usually the by products of thoughts. If you don't like how you're feeling, you might want to change your thinking.

Have you been taking care of your emotions? Consider the choices you have been making. Are they working for or against you?

in this section

Anger

Fun

Happiness

Music

Perspective

Recreation

Relaxation

Sense of Humor

Stress

Stuff

Tears

Vacations

anger

Anger. Daily news reports of child abuse, domestic violence, and aggravated assault make it impossible to ignore. It's clear that someone's anger can seriously harm other people. What we hear less about is the damage it can do the person who is angry.

Anger and hostility can kill us from within. Duke University's Dr. Redford Williams researched the effects of anger on health. He has discovered strong evidence that hostility alone can severely damage the heart. It sends blood pressure skyrocketing and provokes the body to create unhealthy chemicals. "Anger is a poison for hostile people," warns Williams. One study found that angry men in their twenties are seven times more likely to have heart disease or die from a heart attack by age fifty. Hello? Are you paying attention? Have you ever been called a "hot head"? Heads up! This is life-or-death stuff.

If you have a problem with unchecked anger, you already know it. It has probably gotten you into trouble in school, at work, or with people you care about. You've tried to control it but everything just seems to tick you off. After all, you have a right to pitch a fit when people cut you off on the road, don't pull their share of the load, or waste your time. You also have a right to hit yourself in the head with a ball pein hammer. But I wouldn't recommend either. After all, you are the one getting hurt. Do you realize that "blowing your stack" is synonymous with a stroke?

So what can you do? You tried to hold it in, but that just made it worse.

Have you heard the expression "stewing in your own juices"? Just think about what that implies physically. Not a pleasant thought, is it?

The key is to not get angry in the first place. I know that seems like a tall order for someone with a long history of a hair-trigger temper. Just remind yourself that controlling or reducing anger may save your life. Suddenly, it won't be as tough as you thought it was.

Here are some tips from the experts. Learn to slow down. Give yourself a little more breathing space in your day. Do not try to do five things at once. Make a list and just do one thing at a time. Be aware of cynical thoughts and the way you talk to yourself. The world is not a terrible place. Try to give people the benefit of the doubt. (Wouldn't you prefer they did the same for you?) Learn to let things go; carrying a grudge hurts you so much more than the person you are unwilling to forgive. And be nice to yourself, for heaven's sake. Cut yourself some slack whenever you can. Remember that no one is perfect, including you. Do not beat yourself up when you screw up. When mistakes occur, learn to laugh at them and learn from them—then move on!

Before you say, "This just kills me!" remember that it can. Just take a slow deep breath, count to ten, and ask yourself, "Is this worth dying for?" No way. "Is this fight important enough to be my last human inter-action?" I didn't think so. The next time someone tells you to "take it easy," do it! Then thank him. He may have just saved your life.

fun

Fun. If your first thought was "I am too old for that," please take this book and lightly smack yourself in the head. Shame on you! This is the type of thinking that will kill you at forty, even though they may not bury you until seventy-five.

Having fun means doing something for the sole purpose of pure amusement or enjoyment. People's idea of fun varies widely. It may be tinkering around in your workshop, lunching with friends, instigating a neighborhood snowball fight, or crawling back into bed with a good cup of tea and great novel. It all qualifies.

Having fun is a major part of any wellness program because it enhances the quality of our lives. Fun reduces stress levels, improves relationships, and increases our energy. And here is the best part—it's readily available, often free, and usually legal! The important thing to remember is that fun is good (and necessary) for everyone at any age. And, like your favorite vitamins, intervals of fun work best when taken routinely.

In our fast-paced world, taking off "a month of Sundays" just isn't possible. So, why not plan a month of fun-days? That way you'll be sure to find time to play, even during the work week. When you schedule enjoyable activities in advance, your time doesn't get frittered away on piddly little time-consuming activities that add up to nothing. List things you would like to do, just for fun. Be sure to include the big things you want to do before you die on your list—ride a raft down the

Colorado River, organize a gigantic family reunion, or go bungee-jumping—whatever grabs you. Then, identify a lot of things more easily available: Super Bowl parties, hitting garage sales with your best friend, or neighborhood get-togethers for sleigh riding or Frisbee tournaments. Next, list activities you can do all by yourself: long jogs through the park, hours spent quilting, or tinkering on that classic car. Finally, list some activities that you can do with your significant other, kids, grandkids, parents, and so on. How about working on your photo albums, a weekend float trip, or an afternoon at the planetarium? Get your plans made to cover a month-long period. Stick with it, and significant life improvements are guaranteed!

Don't put this off. After all, this is the time of your life. Shouldn't you be having it?

happiness

Happiness.
Lately, something really made me wonder how to define it. It was nothing traumatic like the loss of a friend or exuberantly joyful like a wedding or birth. It was simply a smiley face patch on the back pocket of a boy's jeans. It reminded me that what one person considers happiness, or what makes him happy, may be totally different from anyone else's. I have been looking into that idea and have found some interesting information. It seems that we each develop our own story about what our life should be. We start this process at a young age and gradually add to or edit our story as we grow older. For example, a young girl's story may include finding happiness by marrying a handsome guy and having two perfect children. A young man may feel that a successful career with a high income will result in happiness. People's visions of happiness can be as complex as world peace or as simple as an ice cream cone.

As outside observers, we may conclude that happiness may elude people because their expectations are too high, too narrow, or too rigid. Yet, when it comes to our own stories, we often fail to see them with the same objectivity. The crystal clarity with which we see other's lives seems no match for our lives' permanent haze.

Are your vacation plans ruined because of bad weather? Is your love life disappointing because the soul mate you envisioned has not arrived on the scene? Is your life over because you lost your executive position in a layoff? It happens to the best of us.

Is it possible to influence our own happiness? Absolutely. One way you can do this is to continuously rewrite your story and the expectations you have for your life. Do you wake up disappointed because the day is rainy, or are you simply happy just to have awakened? Are you frustrated that your toddler finger-painted your newly painted wall, or are you happy knowing he is a normal, active three-year-old?

When I was younger, I was certain that I wanted to marry and have children. I had always imagined having four boys. As it turned out, I married much later than I thought I would and gave birth to one beautiful daughter who is all girl. She is a joy and a handful—and I would not trade her for four sons if it gave me 34" hips. The universe obviously had a different plan for me.

My life didn't go exactly the way I had written my story. I did get married and became a mother. I just had to edit the kid part.

Does your story need some editing? Does it have one definitive ending? If so, scrap it! Be open to the excitement of infinite possibilities. This may be a little scary, but isn't your happiness worth it?

Remember, happiness is not based on luck. You have a lot of influence. You, too, can live "happily ever after" if you start finding joy in your life right now. We all know what happens at the end of a fairy tale. What sets one apart from another is the journey it took to get there.

music

Music. It's more than just celebrities trying to earn a buck (or a few million). Personal CD players, stereos, TVs, movie theaters, concert halls—music helps fill the silence of our lives. But did you ever really wonder why we put it there?

Music affects the body, mind, and spirit tremendously. It can stir memories of a senior prom or an especially lonely winter night. Do you get goose bumps during scary movie music, or a lump in your throat when you hear a song that played in a music box your father gave you?

Music can influence the rate of your breathing, blood pressure, muscular tension, and the level of stress hormones in your body. Hospitals and dental offices have taken advantage of these facts for a long time. It's no coincidence that slow, soothing music is often played in crowded waiting rooms, elevators, and even operating rooms. Think about the music that restaurants play. Your neighborhood bar and grill is likely to play country or rock tunes because their patrons tend to be boisterous. They want to unwind and have fun. Restaurants that use crystal and candlelight select music that creates a romantic or peaceful mood. You're likely to hear the Barney songs at places that handle birthday parties for little kids. (If you don't have nerves of steel, I suggest you avoid these places.)

Since music can be so powerful, why not learn to use it to improve your health? Start by paying attention to how music affects you. What styles appeal to you, and at what times? What are you listening to when you realize you are tapping your foot or suddenly feeling a little weepy? You will find certain types genres and songs that cheer you up, reduce your feelings of stress, or mentally take you back to a previous time of life. Others may help get you going in the morning or stir your creative juices. I can think of a CD I own that puts all sleeping pills to shame!

Every teenager knows that music is a great way to escape from the stress of the day. Meanwhile, most adults are too busy yelling, "Turn down that racket!" to remember music's value.

It's time to let go! Pump up the volume. Dance around in your underwear if you feel so inclined. Sing in the car as loudly and dramatically as you please. I promise that the drivers that look at you funny are all just jealous. Do it now. Tune in, and let the good times (rock and) roll.

perspective

Perspective. I really learned the value of it one day when my daughter came home from school, beaming. "Great news, Mom! It's my lucky day. I've been chosen Chairperson of my class."

I don't have to tell you how proud I was. So much so, that it didn't occur to me to question her good fortune—even though she was only four years old at the time. Rather, I was reassured to know that her teacher was so "on the ball" that she recognized the leadership potential in Annie so early in her school career. I had to fight the urge to whip out my Rolodex and call everyone I knew to brag.

When my husband came home, Annie again proudly announced, "Dad, I'm the Chairperson of my class." To my surprise Peter asked, "Just what does the Chairperson do in a room full of four-year-olds?"

"After snack, I put the chairs back under the tables," she answered.

The earth stopped spinning. I stammered, "What are you talking about?"

"See, Mom, there's the Trash Person, the Napkin Person, and the Chair Person. And I'm the Chair Person!" Peter cracked up laughing. I, on the other hand, was thanking my lucky stars that I had refrained from alerting the media of their need to do a featured segment on my child prodigy.

What a lesson in perspective! I believed my child was exceptional, and her being selected to what I thought was a leadership position supported this belief. I never looked for another meaning.

Faulty perspectives are a part of human nature. They can be positive—in my case reminding me that my daughter was special. Or they can be negative—when we notice things that underscore our own belief that we are stupid or klutzy or unappreciated, etc.

It's been said that reality is of our own choosing. What you choose to see can keep you healthy or make you sick. It's your choice. Choose well. And as for me, if my daughter ever comes home announcing she is President, I will be smart enough to ask, "Of what?" before I shout it from the rooftops.

recreation

Recreation. It seems that most of us are suffering from a condition worse than SARS. I am speaking, of course, of chronic burnout. Doesn't a little recreation sound appealing? Think about it. To recreate means to *re-create*—to make new, refresh, restore, or breathe new life into. It's exactly what many of us need.

Although most of us realize the value of recreation, we have trouble doing it. Perhaps it's because we have gotten into the habit of over-scheduling ourselves. We work at a job, we care for a family, and we dedicate ourselves to scads of quests, tasks, and causes. Then, when it's time to play, we're too tired to enjoy it. Sometimes we completely miss the point and make too big a deal of it. Before we have friends over, we feel compelled to clean the entire house and prepare a gourmet meal. By the time our friends leave, we're worn out rather than relaxed. Instead of getting away from everyday life when we go on vacation, we pack half of what we own and drag it with us. Are you guilty of never turning off your cell phone or laptop? It's time to stop defeating your purpose.

What would refresh you? Is it having the next-door neighbors over to watch a good movie? How about a potluck supper where each family in your circle of old friends brings a dish? Maybe you'd enjoy window-shopping—all the sights and sounds of shopping without the credit card bill. Maybe a round of golf at a public course with another duffer.

There are thousands of things we can do for recreation, and many are free. We goof up when we make our recreation too complicated, too expensive, too competitive, or try to squeeze it into an already full day.

It's about time you gave yourself a break. When you do, don't rush to fill up your dance card. I started putting red X's on my calendar to mark days or hours that are as yet unscheduled. This preserves that time for me to do whatever I want with it. Spontaneity is a beautiful thing. When I get to the end of the week and find I would really like to sit on the screened-in porch and watch the sun go down, I can because I haven't overscheduled myself. If a friend calls and asks me to an event, I can honestly say that I have already got something on my calendar. (I do. It's a big red X.) The time is *mine* to fill or fritter away as I choose—a bubble bath, a chance to write my holiday letters, or an evening alone with someone I love.

Leave your schedule open with time available for real recreation. Choose to do things that increase your joy, strengthen your relation-ships, and reduce your stress. Get over the idea that you are wasting your time. You aren't. In only a few hours, you can refresh and restore your life. When is the last time you could say that about a business meeting?

relaxation

Relaxation. Contending with traffic, deadlines, irate customers, teething babies, and noise on a daily basis, we often yell at ourselves, "Relax!" Although our approach is completely counter-productive, we have the right idea. The word "relax" comes from a Latin word meaning "to loosen." Picture someone loosening his collar after a hard day—you almost see muscles around the neck and shoulders releasing, knots in the stomach relaxing, even clenched fists opening up. Relaxation is truly fabulous.

So how *do* you "loosen up"—especially when you don't have a lot of time? One good way to quickly relax is to momentarily fix your attention on sights or sounds that are pleasurable—fish swimming in an aquarium, a colorful sunset, or a single flower. This technique can lower your blood pressure and your heart rate and relax your muscles as well. Nature scenes are especially effective at evoking pleasurable feelings of calm and contentment. They reconnect us with the natural world we evolved to thrive in. And, by diverting our attention outside ourselves, we find ourselves distracted from our usual worries and concerns.

What about watching TV? Isn't that relaxing? Not necessarily. Often what we see is exciting, terrifying, heartbreaking, or depressing. Television shows and movies today are designed to hold our attention by rapidly changing images and sounds. A better choice for calming down might be petting our much-loved cat in front of the fireplace.

In today's fast-paced, mind-boggling world, the peaceful everyday beauty around you is easy to lose sight of. But it's always there! You don't need a garden to stop and smell the roses. Beauty is all around you. Take advantage of it. And, for heaven's sake, loosen up!

sense of humor

A sense of humor. In the long run, it's a lot more beneficial than your sense of style. Unlike the latest designer trends, humor is a natural antidote to stress. Having a sense of humor eases days filled with rush hour traffic, crabby customers, lousy weather, and stacks of unpaid bills. It can also help soothe bigger pains, like a layoff or a divorce. Humor gives us a different way of looking at things that could otherwise be painful, upsetting, or embarrassing.

What is humor? It's the quality that makes something seem funny, amusing, or ludicrous. Where does it come from? Two great sources of humor are our pet peeves and life's little disappointments. Think about this. We don't laugh about perfect children, computers that work beautifully, or an amicable boss. Rather, humor comes from life's little pitfalls—moody teenagers, maddening technology, and grouchy co-workers. We can allow ourselves to get uptight about these things, or we can learn to see the humor. If Jerry Seinfeld and Ray Romano can see humor in everyday life, why can't you?

Have you ever had one of those days when nothing goes right and someone says to you, "Someday you'll look back on this and laugh"? Hello? Big clue here. If you know you're going to look back and laugh, why wait? Learn to laugh about it now.

Laughter is the trademark of humor. You've probably heard the saying, "Laughter is the best medicine." This is very true but not specific enough. The healthful kind of laughter isn't the titter, the little chuckle, or the monosyllabic "Ha." It means the kind of laughter that involves your whole body—the kind that makes your sides hurt and causes tears to roll down your cheeks. You know what I mean. It's the kind of laughter you can't hold in, and the more you try, the harder you laugh. When you finally stop, you find yourself sighing—feeling almost cleansed. It turns out there is a whole lot going on.

Here are just a few of the positive side effects of genuine belly laughter:
- It makes the heart beat faster—an aerobic activity without the spandex or sweat.
- It improves digestion. All that jiggling is like internal jogging.
- It relaxes muscle. Anybody who's ever started laughing while helping to move the neighbor's piano knows that. You have to put it down because you simply can't hold your muscles tight when you're laughing. Warning: laughter relaxes *ALL* your muscles! If you have a full bladder, proceed at your own risk.
- It helps increase immune function. An antidote to stress, laughter has a positive effect on reducing nature's more toxic natural threats.

So far, no one has uncovered any negative effects, aside from temporary incontinence.

Maybe you feel you don't have much reason to laugh. People often say to me, "Nothing funny ever happens to me." or "My life isn't as funny as yours." Honestly, my life isn't any funnier than most people's. It's just that I've learned to seek out people and things that help me to laugh. You can too. Here are a few suggestions:

- Read the comics before the front page. Clip your favorites.
- Select movies and TV programs that make you laugh, not reach for the tissues.
- Make time to be with people with whom you laugh easily. You'll probably find that they have a sense of humor similar to your own. (Avoid grouches and whiners.)
- Start a humor/laughter scrapbook. Save photos, articles, news clippings, ads—anything that you find funny. Humor is everywhere, even on roadside signs in the middle of nowhere (my favorite is EAT AND GET GAS).

Having a sense of humor is like knowing you'll have an umbrella when the rain rolls in. Laughter is the easiest, most enjoyable way to get us through life's rocky periods (and it's a lot cheaper than therapy). If all of the health benefits of a good chuckle could be put in pill form, I'd buy all the stock I could get my hands on. The ability to lighten your life is something you learned before you could even talk. So go on! You have no excuses. Laugh it up!

reflections

Reflections

stress

Stress. It comes to call at the worst possible times. Mine attacked me the other day when I got caught in a doozy of a traffic jam. I was supposed to be at an important meeting, and this delay definitely didn't fit into my plans. I started to stew about the hassle I'd be facing. In no time, I had a classic stress response going on—my heart was pounding, my muscles and stomach were in knots, and mind was going a mile a minute. "This time," I thought, "I won't let stress win."

Taking slow, deep breaths, I started noticing the drivers around me. Several were on their cell phones—conducting business or having romantic conversations. They seemed okay. They had an alternative—something else to do. Five or six people got out of their cars and walked up the highway to see what was going on. They were impatient and obviously irritated over the delay. Did they honestly believe that their presence at the scene would speed things up? But the guy in the car next to me opened his sunroof, turned up his stereo, tipped his seat back, and enjoyed those few moments. Just watching him helped me relax. This was short-lived, however, as I soon heard the sound of two air rescue helicopters lifting off. I knew then that there had been a bad accident. Had we been a few seconds earlier, those of us back here might have been one of the people who were now seriously injured or dead.

Suddenly, the traffic didn't seem so bad. I was okay. I had been granted a little more time. Moreover, I was lucky. These could have been the last moments for any of us. Some of us found alternative ways to use the time beneficially. Some of us wasted it fuming. And one of us used the time to enjoy the stillness, the sunshine, and the music. I want to be that guy!

It's been said, "Stress is not what happens to you, but how you take it." I believe that to be true. How much stress we experience really is our choice. Remember, the odds are good that you could be a lot worse off. Think about that the next time you blow minutes, hours, days, or weeks fretting. Why not go through life like the guy with his seat back and his sunroof open? I guarantee it's a much smoother ride.

stuff

Stuff. We just have to have it and then, when we get it, we either have to clean it, guard it, or keep paying for it long after it's lost its appeal. In our consumer society, our stuff piles up so quickly it seems to be breeding.

George Carlin says, "Home is where you keep your stuff while you're out buying more stuff." Why on earth do we need so much stuff? News flash: we don't. A lot of the things we buy are actually luxuries rather than necessities. "But I need this," you argue. Really? Electric vegetable choppers, leaf blowers, portable footbaths, or the latest fashions (including silk underwear for men)? (Most of the men I know wear their underwear until it falls apart. Silk seems a bit much.) Think about it. If you didn't know the product existed, would you still need it?

We hear so much about these being hard times for people—layoffs, financial insecurity, and the declining value of the dollar. True, these can be stressful times. But we make it worse by constantly accumulating stuff.

You may think I'm making too big a deal of this. If so, try this little exercise and I bet you'll see what I mean. Go around your place and check out everything you have accumulated. Look in the garage, the basement, the attic, the closets, the cabinet, the drawers, and storage locker (gotta love spending your hard-earned money to store things you wasted it on in the first place). Ask yourself, "Could I survive without this?" Be honest. If you're like most of us, you've stockpiled a lot of stuff that you don't even want.

You may want to reduce your stuff or rediscover the stuff you have. Just be wary of accumulating more. Ask yourself if it's worth the amount of hours you'll have to work to pay for it, take care of it, or worry about it. If not, skip it. You'll have more time, fewer credit card bills, less clutter, and maybe the peace of mind that comes with having a little money saved up. Imagine that.

If you have trouble getting rid of "perfectly good stuff," why not donate it to a worthy cause like The Disabled Veterans, Goodwill, The St. Vincent DePaul Society, and the like? Let someone who really could use your things have them. My mother was a quilter and had enough fabric to cover the state. The bumper sticker on her car read, THE ONE WHO DIES WITH THE MOST FABRIC WINS. She was definitely a finalist in the competition. She would never be able to use it all, but couldn't bring herself to part with it. But when we found a woman who made teddy bears for the police and fire departments (who made them available to kids in a crisis), she happily donated tons of her fabric. This greatly reduced her stress, as well as my dad's, and liberated space in their basement they hadn't seen in years.

Speaking of which, we're still wondering what to do with her mayonnaise jar collection. If you have any ideas, please let me know.

tears

Tears. I've got news for you. Big girls (and boys) *do* cry, and for more reasons than over some airhead love interest from the 60s. Of course, many of us shed tears when we're sad or upset. Some of us laugh so heartily that tears stream down our faces. A bunch of us have experienced tearing while chopping raw onions. These tears look the same, but they're not. The tears we cry with emotion, whether in laughter or sadness, contain a chemical that cleanses the eye. Unfortunately, the tears we cry with onions do not. (If they did, onion sales would be up and talk therapy would be out.)

In a time when stress rules, it's understandable why there is a lot of research on tears taking place. It's no longer a surprise to any of us that stress can make us sick. Some tear researchers believe that stress causes the development of a type of toxic waste build-up in our cells. That's right. Stress affects all of you, even your teeniest, tiniest parts. The body needs to rids itself of other waste products or toxins and readjust frequently. Tears are a very effective way of doing just that. I remember hearing a counselor say, "Go ahead and cry it out of your system." I assumed then that the "it" I was supposed cry out was my case of the blues. I know now that she must have meant the toxins. What a wise lady, huh?

Think back to a time you when you felt frustrated, anxious, angry, or sad, and you had what's commonly referred to as a "good cry." I'll bet you felt better afterward. But why? The circumstances that caused your tears probably hadn't changed. It was the sheer fact of crying and the act of shedding tears that helped you to regain your emotional balance. And here's the really great news! Tears that accompany laughter bring the same type of relief and rebalancing. Isn't that terrific?

So go see a sad movie and bawl your eyes out. Hit the comedy clubs and laugh until the tears flow. Hey, I'll bring the tissues.

vacation

Vacation. "It's the only thing that there's just too little of." And you thought that it was "love, sweet love"? Nope, I'm talking about ski slopes, drinks with little umbrellas in them, and romantic sunsets.

Most of us look forward to vacations more than anything else—especially when the weather is lousy and the workweek seems endless. And with good reason. Webster's Dictionary defines vacation as "a period of rest" and "freedom from work." But here's a question: Why, then, do so many people need a vacation *after* their vacation?

I have a few ideas. We say a vacation is a chance to "get away from it all," and then we pack it up and take it all with us. I see minivans bulging with kids, animals, and enough luggage for six months. I see RVs the size of condominiums, complete with satellite dishes, full kitchens, and mini-offices. It's hard to find a serene wilderness area without rock music blaring and microwaves beeping. And we wonder why we can't unwind?

Before you take your next vacation, think about what you really need. Listen to your body. Listen to your heart. Do you need unstructured time to reflect, sleep in, or do without noise for a while? Would that feel great? Maybe you're a little bored and need the stimulation of new sights, interesting people, and exciting experiences.

My family and I rented a house in Hawaii during one spring break. Rather than follow any schedule or regimen, we decided not to use watches or clocks. We went to bed when our bodies felt like sleeping. We woke up naturally, rather than to the jarring sound of an alarm clock. It took a few days for each of us to really settle into our natural biorhythms. Not surprisingly, my teenager's sleep cycle was way different from the middle-aged adults'. Consequently, someone in the family was up before the birds, while another rolled out of bed at the crack of noon. It was wonderful, though, because it felt so right for each of us. There was no pressure to conform or compromise with someone else's needs. It reduced stress enormously and limited battles to only the really important things—like custody of the pool.

Vacations are supposed to rejuvenate us—to relieve stress, to rebuild energy, and to regain a better perspective. And they can—if we don't lose sight of their purpose. This year, don't return to your cubicle wishing you had another two weeks off to recover from your vacation. Do it right the first time. Use what little time you have to really let go and enjoy yourself. Bon voyage!

reflections

Reflections

emotional health

reflections

Reflections

social h

relating to your relationships

Think of the people in your life and the effect they have on your sense of well-being. Do you feel connected, supported, and loved? Do you experience a sense of fellowship and community? Or do you feel isolated or lonely? Do you think people don't understand you or have let you down?

Have you been taking care of your relationships? Consider the choices you have been making. Are they working for or against you?

in this section

Celebrations
Friendship

Gift Giving
Intimacy
Just Say "No"
Just Say "Yes"
Keeping in Touch
Life
Marriage
Pets
Roots
Smiling

celebrations

Celebrations. Your birthday, New Year's Eve, Flag Day—
these days are known for their celebrations (well maybe not Flag Day
so much). They give us time to slow down, appreciate things, and
have a little fun. One of my favorites happens yearly, when my husband,
Peter, and I commemorate our wedding anniversary at one of the best
restaurants in town. It's become our tradition. With magnificent service
and superb food, the evening is unhurried, quiet, and romantic. We
always talk about the events of our lives over the past year, as well as
our hopes and goals for our new year together.

Now I know some of you are thinking that an evening like this is a
waste of money. A gift would last longer. After such an evening, what
do you have? Well, I'll tell you. You have honored your past,
strengthened your bonds, renewed your commitment to each other,
and you've added good stuff to the mental memory book of your lifetime. I'd say that's worth a little bit of extra work.

Sadly, many people forego celebrations. They say fancy-schmancy
parties are too much trouble. Why get out the good china when you
can use paper plates? Why put up the Christmas tree for only a week?
Why wrap birthday gifts when the kids will just rip off the paper and
you'll wind up pitching it? Why go to all that trouble? What's the big
deal? As my father always says, "It's just another day."

No, it's not! Celebrations help us pay attention to the truly important
things in life. It's good to slow down, to share quality time with family

or friends. What most people don't understand is that your traditions don't have to be china and crystal. They can be family barbeques, popping popcorn and watching home movies on the first snowy night of the year, or reading the comics in bed on Sunday mornings. It's great to throw a party for momentous occasions, but it's also fun to hit the water park on the first day of summer vacation. The opportunities are endless.

Not enough celebrating in your own life? Consider how you might help others commemorate their special happenings. Present your niece with the video you shot as she was awarded her master's degree. Plan a shopping trip to celebrate a friend's successful loss of forty pounds. Hold a "puppy shower" to acknowledge your neighbor's first litter of Yorkies. It doesn't matter what the activity is, as long as it's fun and brings people together.

My mother left this world at the age of eighty-seven. She lived with my family for the last nine years of her life. Rather than the usual remembrances of floral arrangements or tuna casseroles, my neighbors got together and gave us a glorious redbud tree in her honor. One afternoon we all assembled around the tree and christened it with champagne while toasting the wonderful woman she was. I will never forget that celebration. Every time that I see that tree I think of my mother and feel grateful to have such wonderful neighbors.

The world of the twenty-first century can seem impersonal, rushed, and even scary at times. It's easy to get caught up in the news, the daily grind, or the hassles of the day. Sometimes we need to stop and acknowledge our blessings.

Celebrations and traditions strengthen our relationships. They connect us. They help us to feel like we belong, giving us a better sense of who we are and where we fit in the grand scheme of things.

The Mad Hatter had the right idea when he wished Alice "a very merry un-birthday!" So what if it's not your anniversary or a national holiday? Celebrate today. After all, isn't the everyday beauty of life cause enough?

reflections

Reflections

friendship

Friendship. The best definition of "friend" I've ever heard is this: *Someone who really knows you and likes you anyway.* I am truly blessed to have so many of these exceptional someones. Many of them are of the "those that knew me when" variety—friends who came into my life during my childhood and my high school and college years. My list of friends also includes my work buddies, married couple chums, and pals from my neighborhood. (I also belong to a group called "The Bad Girls," but we won't go into that here.)

Every one of them has distinctly different personalities and talents. Some of my friends are real characters. Although no two are anywhere near alike, they are naturally funny and extremely entertaining. Year after year, they continue to crack me up. Friends are perfect providers of a good laugh or swift kick in the keester.

I have other friends who challenge me. They encourage me to develop my skills and broaden my horizons. I like the way they stimulate my mind. I can feel myself stretch my abilities when I am around them. Their faith in my talents prompts me to take more professional risks.

Finally, there are my very closest friends, who form my personal support patrol. They listen to me when I need to vent. They are instinctively there when I don't want to be alone. And they have the guts to give honest advice when I ask for their opinions. (Best of all, they try to be diplomatic when letting me know that I'm over the top, have bitten off more than I can chew, or am acting like a woman in need of prescriptive sedative.) What a comfort it is to know that I am understood and appreciated for the person I truly am!

Friends are priceless treasures that should never be taken for granted. Friendships need to be cultivated and nurtured. They require our time and attention, valuable commodities in these hurried times. But simple things like a phone call, a silly card sent snail mail, a good gab over the backyard fence, or even a quick walk around the block together can strengthen the bonds of friendship.

Having good friends keeps us healthy and sane. They are as important as exercise and good nutrition. Don't wait until you need them to appreciate them. I would talk more about this, but I've got a good friend on the phone and I don't want to miss a moment. Besides, friendship's value is clearest when your own special people surround you. So get off the couch and pick up the phone! Your friends are waiting.

gift giving

Gift Giving.
Nowadays, it seems like the gift that keeps on *costing*. It seems to have become obligatory, or a real burden, for a lot of folks. I hear people saying, "I've got six more gifts I *have* to buy," rather than, "There are six people I'd love to do something for." This type of gift giving feels like a requirement and a chore. You trudge through the mall trying to find the perfect gift *for the man who has everything*. (If he already has everything, why am I trying to give him more?) Half the time the mindset is: *Since he gave me something, I have to give him something back.* That's crazy, pure and simple.

The economy can stink. Times can be tough. A lot of people simply don't have the extra cash for anything but necessities. Nevertheless, many will still go into debt buying things for others that they neither need nor want. On top of it, we often feel that gifts are required for our immediate family just because it's Father's Day, Grandparent's Day, Veterans Day, Valentine's Day, Secretary's Day, and Little Billie's First Lost Tooth Day. (Okay, a dime under the pillow probably won't break the bank, although I've heard some Tooth Fairies are leaving ten bucks these days. In the interest of keeping this book to less than five hundred pages, I won't go there. However, I would like to thank those of you who are doing this for making me look cheap.) Enough already. All this gift giving is self-inflicted stress at its best.

Mark Twain made an astute observation. He said, "Most people spend money they don't have, to buy things they don't need, to impress people they don't like."

If you're nodding in agreement, it's time to make some changes. Try this. Before you buy something for someone, ask yourself, *Am I doing this because I should or because I really want to?* "Should" is a red flag. If you "want" to do something for someone, rethink what you have to give. Maybe your time or talent would be better appreciated than a store-bought gift that isn't needed.

Consider giving personal "gift certificates" for your services to friends and family. My mom used to give us coupons for a full weekend of babysitting so that my husband and I could get away without worry or childcare expense. That gift was a genuine treat that meant a lot to us. How about giving your grandparents a coupon for cleaning their garage or basement? Offer a friend a coupon for a special homemade dessert to be delivered in time for a party she's hosting.

Giving of one's time and talent is giving done in the spirit of love, not just giving because you feel you should. It doesn't take much money, if any—just a little time and talent. And that beats a receiving twelve-gauge Salad Shooter any day!

intimacy

Intimacy. Now don't start picturing trashy romance novel men and beds covered with rose petals. I'm talking about intimacy in its broader sense: the kind that comes with sharing part of our true, deeper selves with another human being. In this context, we can share intimate relationships with many people—of any age or gender. (Imagine that: something today that isn't driven by sex.)

We hear a lot about loneliness. It seems that so many of us feel isolated or disconnected. Sometimes, we try to correct that feeling by surrounding ourselves with crowds of people or lots of activity, only to find that we wind up feeling even lonelier. Why is that? It's because we aren't really close to these people, and therefore we don't feel comfortable sharing our true selves with them. These relationships are superficial at best.

The best relationships are based on openness, honesty, and trust. To some, the whole idea of that type of relationship is scarier than baring your soul on *Jerry Springer*. We worry about becoming too vulnerable. Face it. You will. But nine times out of ten, the benefits will far outweigh the risks and the hassles.

Make sure you have people in your life you trust and feel close to. These people may include an old friend, a coworker, your spouse, a family member, or a spiritual advisor. We need to be able to share our problems, worries, and difficulties, as well as our joys and triumphs.

Choose several so you that you don't put all you eggs in one basket. Everyone knows that nothing gets us over the loss of a significant other like a circle of friends (not even ice cream and a Doris Day marathon). They serve as our anchor by keeping us connected and on an even keel when life gets rough.

Remember, friendship is a two-way street. In order to take, we also must give. It's important to remember that no one is perfect. We all have our good qualities and bad qualities. They come as part of the package. Sharing ourselves with others—our strengths and weaknesses, our joys and sorrows—is the antidote to loneliness. Choosing to share your gifts with others is mutually beneficial. Intimacy doesn't have to be a dirty word. So get out there and get intimate (no muscle-bound hunks or damsels in distress required!).

just say "no"

"No." We all know (and most of us dislike) a "Yes-man" in our lives. It drives us crazy that he (or she) agrees to everything without a second thought. But can you relate? It's so hard for some of us to simply say, "No." We feel put on the spot. Because we are uncomfortable saying "no," we wind up doing all kinds of things we really don't want to do. Whether it's spending our birthdays with our spouse's bass-fishing buddies, pet sitting for the neighbor's slobbering St. Bernard, or giving up a much-needed day of rest, being unable to say "no" can create a lot of stress.

Sure, donating time to a worthy cause can be good for you if it's done in the spirit of love. But, if your teeth are clenched and a knot is beginning to form in the pit of your stomach, take heed. On those occasions, listen to your body and, to quote Nancy Reagan, "Just say no."

I know you're squirming. How can you refuse to be a bridesmaid in a former college roommate's wedding (even though you've been out of school for decades, it's her fourth marriage, and the wedding is in Guam)? How can you pass up the chance to coach your four-year-old's roller-hockey team, especially when the other dads aren't nearly as athletic as you are? Shouldn't you show your in-laws, once and for all, that Martha Stewart has nothing on you when it comes to throwing a party? No, no, no . . . Get over it!

Years ago I learned an easy and effective way to say no. The formula is *two positives, a negative, and a positive.* It works like this: "Kathy, will you be in charge of the chili supper/fundraiser for underprivileged gerbils this year?" "Gee," I say, "That's a really big job (positive), and I'm flattered you think I could handle it (positive). Unfortunately, I'm not available that day (negative). Thanks for thinking of me (positive)." *Two positives, a negative, and a positive.* Did that sound offensive? No. Did I tell why I wasn't available? No! That's the key. Don't make up excuses or feel compelled to justify your decision.

I'm not suggesting that you never get involved. Giving your time and talent can be good for your health. But, if you're already in charge of the local Girl Scout troop and deliver meals to shut-ins, someone else can be in charge of the Flag Day Pageant.

You can't give away what you don't have. You need time to take care of yourself and your family. Get your priorities straight. Remember, you have a choice; and every now and then it's okay to say "no."

just say "yes"

Yes. Remember that word? It's the opposite of our favorite word, "no." It's easy to forget about when you hear the expression "Just say no" a hundred times a day. I realize it was coined to help young people deal with the drug and alcohol issue. Now, in that context, I think it's great to just say "no." But I've noticed how often we say "no" or other negative things to kids. I'm not sure that's so great.

In one study, children four and under wore tape recorders throughout the day to determine how much positive input they received. The results were dismal. Something like 85% of what was said to kids was negative: "Don't touch." "Quit that." "Put that down." "Be quiet." "Stop it." "You're such a mess." "Can't you do anything right?"

These days we hear a lot of negative things about our young people: questionable morals, declining scores on standardized tests, overall laziness, a lack of direction, and poor self-esteem are a few items on their list of flaws. Is it any wonder? Maybe if 85% of what we said to our kids was positive, we could change things for the better.

If you have children of your own or have contact with children, why not try the positive? "Yes, you can." "Yes, I'll tell you a story." "Yes, you can try on my lipstick." "Yes, you can invite a friend along." "Yes, I'll look over your homework." "Yes, I'm proud of you." I have a feeling that if even 50% of what our kids heard was positive, it might make a big difference. Of course, it'll take conscious effort and will often be time consuming or inconvenient. I'm certainly not suggesting you cancel your children's curfew, double their allowance, or let them off the hook about getting decent grades, but I'm betting the payoff from some well-timed affirmatives will be well worth the effort.

I talk a lot about wellness and happiness and quality of life—for kids as well as adults. It is my belief that we can improve the health, happiness, and quality of life of young people (and us older geezers too) by learning to say "yes" more often than "no." Think of it as language karma. If you put out positive energy, it will return to you. So, do as Mother always told you, and "watch your mouth!" When you consider the outcome, it seems like a pretty good idea, yes?

Keeping in touch

"Keep in touch." That expression gets a lot of lip service. "Stay in touch, now." "We'll be in touch." Yeah, right. Half the time, that's the end of it. But every now and then people actually follow through, and it's surprising and wonderful!

I love getting letters, phone calls, and e-mails from old friends whom I haven't seen in years. Hearing about new babies, career moves, and family vacations help me feel that, even though our lives have gone in different directions, we are still connected. Some of my friends and relatives send pictures. Others add newspaper clippings or a newsletter. Whatever it is, I enjoy it all.

Life is so hectic these days. Although we have good intentions of getting together for lunch or calling someone in order to catch up, the days go by. We don't manage to get around to it. We get wrapped up in trivial things or the endless routine of everyday life. If we run into a friend at the grocery store or hair salon we say, "We really should get together. Call me." We mean it when we say it. We just don't follow through. And where do we run into them next? Funerals! Then what do we say to them? "I wish we could have seen each other under happier circumstances. Anyway, we ought to get together!"

Isn't a funeral a gigantic clue that time on this planet isn't infinite? We shouldn't put off spending time with people we love or whose company we truly enjoy. Isn't this more important than mundane activity? After all, the gift of friendship is priceless.

Who are the significant people in your life? How often do you think of them? What happy memories do you share? Why not take a few minutes to give them a call, write them a letter, or arrange a get-together? Keep in touch. Odds are you'll say it to someone very soon. Before you let it slip out of your mouth and out of your life, make a pact with yourself that you'll see to it. That way, at the next funeral, you won't be dwelling on things you didn't do. Just get out there and do them!

life

Life. It's an overwhelming thing to contemplate, but the other day it seemed very simple.

An SUV passed me on the highway. The dad was driving. Three young kids were climbing over the back seat into the cargo area to wave at cars and try to get truck drivers to honk. The mom sat in the front seat, holding a baby on her lap. Their bumper sticker read, PRECIOUS CARGO. In a split second, my feelings about life became very clear: *Precious . . . a gift . . . a very fragile one.* I wanted to scream, "Buckle those kids in!"

It's baffling. If you ask parents-to-be whether they want a boy or a girl, nine out of ten times the answer is, "We don't care, so long as the baby is healthy." We all pray for ten fingers and ten toes, hearts that beat, and brains that can think. When our prayers are answered, we jeopardize that life by failing to use car seats and seat belts.

I worked in pediatrics for a long time. I have known kids who were thrown from cars or who hit the dashboard. Many of them will never walk, speak, or recognize their parents again.

I notice teenagers laughing and talking as they pile into a car. Often they drive away without anyone bothering to put on a seat belt. I'm not embarrassed to tell you that I'm one of those people who waves the kids down in parking lots (much to their surprise) and reminds them that the law requires seat belts, and that life does too. I also tell adults in the neighborhood when I see their kids tooling around unsecured. You can call me a busybody or a snitch, but I figure it's better than doing nothing and hearing about a tragedy later.

Sadly, going without seat belts isn't the only way we jeopardize our lives and the lives of those we love. Start paying attention to the risks you take. Do you drive too fast? Drink and drive? Misuse medication? Bike without a helmet? Leave flammable substances in inappropriate places? Smoke? Refuse to tell anyone about your recurring chest pain? Avoid breast self-examination and Pap smears? You add to this list. I know you can.

Forget the excuses. They pale in comparison to the risk. Dead or alive? Much of the time it's your choice. We are responsible for the health and happiness of ourselves *and* of those we love. It takes a whole village to raise a child and that village can also help make his life worth living. Cherish the miracle of life . . . and in the meantime, buckle up!

marriage

Marriage. Wow, is my husband lucky to have me! No kidding. I was reading a study that found married men live longer than single men. Oh, I can just hear the male response, "It's not longer, it just seems longer." Nope. Sorry, guys. The fact remains, it IS longer.

I wondered why this is true. Is it because married men have cleaner clothes and, therefore, fewer germs around? Perhaps it was because they were forced to eat veggies, show up at church, or had wives who made them drive slower and wear seat belts.

Longevity doesn't have to do with those things at all. It has to do with love. That's right. The study indicated that being loved provides men with some type of umbrella of protection that keeps them from getting sick as often. And, if they do become ill, they recover more quickly.

It's really not so far-fetched. Think about it for a few minutes. We know that the stresses in our daily lives are bad for health and longevity. But, isn't it stress relieving to know that someone who *really* knows you—pot-gut, receding hairline, bad habits, and all—loves you anyway?

I don't believe it works as effectively if you have to assume that you're loved. Love is most valuable when we express our feelings to our beloved through our words and actions. Maybe it's a special breakfast in bed once in a while. Perhaps it's cheerfully attending a spouse's event of choice that you'd really rather miss. (Okay, I draw the line at monster truck rallies—no offense if that's your "thing.") It may be as simple as sitting on the porch and holding hands while watching the sun go down. Hearing the words "I love you, Babe" never gets old if it's true.

Now we're investigating the benefits of all kinds of loving relationships with significant others and friends. Time will tell, but I believe the news will be good.

Genuine love is good medicine for body, mind, and spirit. It's not always easy to find, and it should be nurtured and cherished when you do. So, is my husband lucky to have me? You'd better believe it. (I remind him of that before every anniversary.) And I'm lucky, too. We keep each other well. Now that's love!

pets

Pets. They are on my mind, because as I write this, our little Yorkshire terrier, Kramer, is lying on top of my desk, sleeping so soundly that I am wondering if he might be unconscious.

Animals are interesting creatures—so much so, that we often choose to live with them, despite the fact they can bite us, scratch us, disrupt our sleep, and ruin our carpeting.

Why do we put up with the cost and inconvenience of a pet? Is it worth the hassle? Interestingly enough, for many people, owning a pet may be a lifesaver. Now, you're probably picturing the Lassie look-alike who nudges his owner awake, thereby saving the entire family from a gas leak. That's not quite what I mean.

Research on the effects of owning a pet indicates that pets can reduce our stress by distracting us from our own problems. It's hard to sit and feel sorry for yourself when the dog has to go out NOW. And the unconditional love we get from a pet is heart-warming. Fluffy doesn't care about your midriff bulge or wrinkles. Spanky doesn't think you're a nerd. Perhaps one of the most surprising findings was that pet owners who suffered a heart attack had one-fifth the death rate of people who didn't own pets.

On the surface, you might guess it's because pet owners have to get out and walk more. But birds, cats, fish, and hamsters don't require us to exercise them. So what is it? Maybe it's talking our problems over with Tweetie, or the relaxation we feel watching fish swim in their tank. Both can lower blood pressure. There is some evidence to indicate that the sense of total responsibility for some living thing other than oneself may provide the incentive to stay alive.

The reasons aren't all clear, but the statistics can't be denied. Taking care of your pet may not be as one sided as you think. It may be the other way around. Looks like Rover really might be "man's best friend" after all.

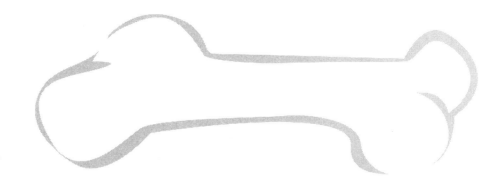

roots

Roots.   Not the kind we associate with trees (although that's a good analogy) but rather the kind we associate with family.

Family roots should be very important to us. They give us a sense of history. They help us to know more about who and where we came from. They give us ideas of what we might expect of ourselves. Understanding our roots helps us to feel connected in an otherwise large and frightening world.

Nothing helps us get in touch with our roots more than family stories. It's often through these that we hear about a family that was courageous enough to come here from another country, strong enough to withstand hardship and disappointment, creative enough to start a business, or silly enough to play practical jokes on each other.

What are you doing to strengthen your family's sense of roots? Do you keep family photographs in view? Do you have keepsakes of special events in the lives of family members? (Awards, postcards, embarrassing home movies?) Do you talk about family members in ways that are memorable or comparative? "I'll never forget the day the twins were born." "In that dress you look just like your grandmother." "Tommy is as clever as a fox, just like Uncle David." "You have Aunt Fran's beautiful brown eyes."

Make it a point to record and pass on valuable information—like medical history. Also, be sure to record interesting information—the most exciting thing that ever happened in the family, the special talents family members have had, the kinds of beliefs that were held. This is wonderful stuff. It helps us to feel grounded. It gives us a foundation.

My mother was the one in our extended family who kept our history alive. She knew the personality styles, occupations, spouses, kids, diseases, and idiosyncrasies of everybody. As she set a Christmas table with her grandmother's Havilland china, she could tell the story about how it was brought to Colorado from Ireland and was used anytime another pioneer family stopped by. She could identify unmarked photos, knick knacks, and war decorations. One of the best things I ever did was help Mom record all her thoughts and information before she left the planet. She gifted generations to come by preserving this information on our roots (and made grade school genealogy projects a lot easier for my daughter).

Take advantage of today's technology. Use digital cameras, video recorders, and the Internet to record and research your family history.

The next time Grandpa starts to share his "I walked five miles to school every day in the snow" story, don't be too quick to groan or remind him that both ways couldn't possibly be uphill. Rather, pull up a chair. Listen. Ask questions. Then share things about your life as well. Think of it as a little fertilizer for the roots that will last you a lifetime.

smiling

Smiling. Recently, I received a photograph of an old acquaintance in the mail. A professional photographer had taken the picture, and my friend was smiling. I didn't recognize her for several minutes. She had the same haircut and hadn't had any plastic surgery but I don't ever remember seeing her smile.

I could just imagine her sitting under the camera lights while the photographer cheerfully directed, "Smile." She obliged momentarily—and I have a feeling that was the end of that. Too bad, because she looks a lot better when she smiles.

I'm afraid she is like a lot of people who don't smile much any more. It's not that anything is wrong—it's just that nothing is especially right. They don't have a particular reason to smile, or they think they need to feel good BEFORE they smile. Actually, it's the other way around. Smiling makes us feel better because it affects the chemistry of the body in a positive way. It's a neat built-in feature we all have. Give it a shot. Go around smiling for a few minutes. At first it seems an eternity, but you'll get used to it, and you'll find your mood improves. Why? Because smiling is a behavior of a happy person. When you're smiling, the brain says, "Hey, I must be happy," and you start to feel better. Sounds a little crazy, but I kid you not.

If it's so great, why don't we smile more? If you are female, especially in the workplace, you might be afraid people will think you're a flirt or an airhead. If you're a male, you may think it looks unprofessional or wimpy. I couldn't disagree more.

Try a little experiment. For the next few days, smile and nod briefly at everyone you see. At first people may wonder what you're up to (especially if you call New York City your home). But eventually, I bet you'll find that people start to smile back at you. And then a nice thing happens. They feel better too. They start going around smiling more and affect other people—who then smile more. It's contagious in a good way!

What have you got to lose? Start right this minute! Don't wait for some photographer to say, "SMILE." Do it on your own. It may totally change the way you look and feel. Who knows, you may not even recognize yourself. I promise it'll be a change that will be worth getting used to.

reflections

Reflections

reflections

Reflections

vocation

relating to your work or "calling"

You may work for a paycheck or you may have chosen to be a stay-at-home caregiver. Whatever you do, think about the effect your work has on the quality of your life. Does your work help fulfill your needs? Does it provide you with good food, a safe place to live and a sense of security? Does it give you a sense of value and opportunities to grow your skills and contribute your talents? Or do you feel a sense of drudgery or boredom? Are you just showing up and going through the motions?

Have you been taking care of your work life? Consider the choices you have been making. Are they working for or against you?

in this section

Appreciation
Attitude
Body of Work

Business or Pleasure?
Competition
Harvest
Recess
Reflection
Service
Speak Up!
Work
You

appreciation

Appreciation. I don't mean to brag, but I'm still feeling proud of myself because of a standing ovation I got last night. No kidding. I gave a presentation, and the audience stood up and applauded me. It was fabulous! It felt great to be so well received, so appreciated. Half a day later, I'm still glowing.

I work in a business in which applause is considered appropriate feedback for a job well done. As a professional speaker, I've been lucky and have received it often. Let me tell you, any applause is nice, but when you get a genuine standing ovation it's a reward you remember for a long time.

This isn't limited to my profession. Watch professional football players score a touchdown. They do a little end-zone dance, strut around, and share high-fives and chest-bumps with their teammates as the fans cheer wildly. Pay attention when baseball players score a crucial run or pitch a final strike. They are surrounded by fellow players, hoisted up on shoulders, and paraded around the infield like conquering heroes. Olympic champions have medals placed around their necks with great pomp and pageantry. These signs of appreciation are as clear as day.

It's a shame that everyone can't experience this kind of appreciation every now and then. Think about what it would mean to a school bus driver who delivers rowdy kids safely home in the snow; or to a janitor who repeatedly mops up the slush from the building foyer to keep employees from falling; or to the electric company road crews who work at all hours to keep our homes warm and well lit. It doesn't have to be a standing ovation, but I'll bet that a word of thanks or a note expressing genuine appreciation would go a long way.

Just think about that word "appreciate." If your house or investments appreciate, they increase in value. Why limit the hurrahs to the athletes, performers, or politicians? The next time you find value in the efforts of others, let them know. Make it a big deal, too. A little appreciation can go a long way. Conveying your gratitude increases others' sense of value; and that's a pretty cool thing to do. Besides, if what goes around really does come around, someone along the way is bound to return the favor. Wouldn't that be nice?

attitude

Attitude. One day I overheard my daughter's friend saying, "Oooh girl, that boy has got some attitude!" It didn't necessarily mean that he had a bad attitude. Younger people use the word to mean "presence," or a strong sense of self.

What's your attitude? How do you feel about yourself, and how does it come across? I know you know what I'm talking about. I'm asking you to think about what your "affect" is.

This will probably be easier if you first start by thinking about someone else. Envision one of your coworkers. Try one you have never been able to warm up to. Why do you think that is? What about that person turns you off? What is his affect? His external attitude? Is he cocky? Does he come across as a know-it-all? Do you get the impression he thinks he's better than everyone else? If so, where are you getting that impression? Does he butt in to the discussion, asserting his unsolicited opinion? Does he put down ideas generated by other members of the team? Does he lead people to believe he's privy to information others don't have?

Now think about a coworker you really like working with. What's the difference between her and the guy I just described? In what ways does her "attitude" make you feel totally different? Is her personality consistently warm and open? Is she open to suggestions and apt to give compliments? Does she defer to others when they have ideas to share? Does she share the glory but takes the blame?

In the workplace, your body is a billboard for your attitude. It tells people loud and clear what your "internal attitude" is. We call it body language. The swagger, the wide grin, the yawn—all messages letting others know we're paying attention, we're bored, or we think we're God's gift to the company.

Now ask yourself how others would describe *your* "attitude." What would you like them to say? Approachable, fair, enthusiastic, open-minded, a great listener?

Pay attention to how you come across. You might even ask a respected colleague or confidant for his or her opinion.

It's important information because it will tell you whether you are inadvertently opening or closing doors, missing out on opportunities, or giving good vibes to people who can help you go places with your career. So often we get into a type of "personality rut." We demonstrate the same behavior at weekly team meetings or with our customers.

If you're not getting the results you want, take a few minutes and check out your attitude.

You don't want to be coming across as a fussbudget when deep down you're really mild mannered. Why hold back your best ideas and have people think you're dumb when you know you're brilliant? (Just a tip: make sure you're radiating "brilliant" and not "cocky.")

Get cracking. Spiff up your "attitude." There's an idea you can take to the bank!

body of work

A body of work. Who is the first person that pops into your head in conjunction with that phrase? Most people immediately think of people famous for their art forms—Beethoven, Shakespeare, Picasso. Others imagine the great scientific minds of Edison, Einstein, or Franklin. Maybe you thought of Mother Theresa, Reverend Martin Luther King, or Gandhi. I'm betting most of you thought of someone other than yourself. Am I right? Granted, these folks have made wonderful contributions to the world, but it's a mistake to think that you have to be an artist, an inventor, an athlete, or a celebrity of some kind in order to have a body of work.

I knew a nun from Italy who had been sent to the United States to teach with other Sisters from her order. Unfortunately, Sister Filicetta's English was never good enough to work in a high school classroom. She was given the assignment of working in a day care with preschool kids, a role she joyfully accepted. Years later, I can still remember her amazing smile and warm hugs. For generations, her unconditional love for her charges, day after day, year after year, had an enormous impact on the lives of those children she called her "bambinos." She told me it was her tiny piece of the world to care for. Her years of service were her body of work.

My life has been made easier because of two wonderful women who have helped me along the way. Every two weeks for almost twenty years, Marie has helped me clean my house. I call her "the cleaning fairy." Her dependability, positive energy, and incredibly thorough work are exceptional. In all these years, she's never complained about how messy my family is (which is truly amazing). I swear that if she ever retires, I'm selling my house and moving to a motel!

Another of my personal angels, Carol, came to our home to help care for my mother when Mom could no longer be safely left alone. She was just what the doctor ordered—flexible, patient, and a great listener—often hearing the same stories again and again. Carol would fix Mom's hair and paint her nails. On days Mom felt well enough to get out, they'd make an afternoon of going to the library and getting a soft serve ice cream. Now that Mom has left the planet, Carol often dog sits for my Yorkie, Kramer, since I can't bear to kennel him when I'm on the road. This not only thrills the dog, it keeps my guilt level down.

These terrific gals have become members of our family.
Their contributions to our quality of life cannot be
denied. I'm sure the other families they've helped
would agree that they have a body of work
they can be proud of.

It comes down to consistently
trying to do your best in
order to make a positive
difference or offer
something of value to
others as well as to yourself. Whether you're a jet
pilot or a janitor, a baker or a brain
surgeon, work on an
assembly line or in
the front line,
there will come a
time when you
look back and take
stock of your work.
Your contribution
needn't be a cure for
cancer. It might be decades of
service with a smile, consistent

quality for a fair price, or the
ability to make the workplace enjoyable for others.

Never discount your value. Before you start your job
today, take a moment to consider how you might add to
the legacy that is your body of work. When the day is
done, look back on the good work you've done and be
proud of it. Pat yourself on the back and go pamper
yourself a little. You've earned it.

business or

"Business or pleasure?" "Come again?" I asked the hotel clerk who had posed the question. "Does your trip involve business or pleasure?" he clarified. "Gee, I didn't know it had to be one or the other. Can't I combine the two?" He laughed and said, "Sounds like a good idea, but to tell you the truth, I don't see many people do it." Sadly, I had to agree with him.

Somewhere along the way we've been conditioned to believe that work and play are opposites. Everyone knows what T.G.I.F. stands for—Thank God It's Friday! The implication being, now that the weekend is here, I can enjoy myself. As for the rest of the week, having fun at work is the same as goofing off: pleasure needs to be reserved for the times we're not on the clock.

Sorry, Charlie. Wrong answer. If there is no pleasure in your work life, how can you possibly do a good job? You can't, plain and simple. However, seek out opportunities for pleasure while you're working and you'll find endless benefits for yourself, your coworkers, and those you meet in the course of your work. I'm talking about higher energy, better attitudes, more creative ideas, stronger teamwork, greater satisfaction, and more desirable outcomes!

Suddenly, the pleasure you used to think of as the anti-work is sounding pretty productive, huh? Great news: combining it with business is easy! Start by pinpointing what you don't like about your work. Are you a "people person" in a job with little human contact? If so, maybe *pleasure?*

being the receptionist would be more fun than the transcriptionist. Do you suffer from the midday blues? Pry yourself away from that riveting game of solitaire, emerge from your cubicle, and eat with some of your more upbeat coworkers. If you're feeling extra motivated, why not organize a weekly outdoor volleyball game? Open it up to anyone in the company who wants to join in. (If you're not feeling extra moti-vated, go back and re-read the "Motivation" piece, you slacker).

Business travelers are often the worst when it comes to adding a little pleasure to their day. They wrap themselves in an invisible cocoon and miss every opportunity for enjoyment available to them. With cell phones glued to their ears, they are oblivious to the sights and sounds around them. On the plane, they anxiously await the announcement that it's safe to turn on their laptops, on which they will fixate the entire trip. Personally, I'd rather dive into a great book, take a little snooze, or discover the interesting person seated next to me. Whenever I fly, it always amazes me how people keep their noses to the grindstone rather than pressed against the window. I asked one worka-holic seatmate if he'd like to switch seats with me so that he could enjoy the spectacular views of the Grand Canyon. His response? "I've already seen it!" Sheesh! Ok, buddy. Sorry I asked.

My husband was sent to work in Greece for

ten weeks. He took advantage of the opportunities the assignment presented to him. On his off hours, he met wonderful people as he explored the city, found charming tavernas for dinner each evening, and dove into the richness of the history. On weekends he took a ferry to breathtaking islands like Santorini and

Mykonos. He was dumbfounded that so many of his teammates sat gathered around a black-and-white TV in the hotel lobby, bemoaning the fact that they couldn't get a decent hamburger!

However, you don't have to travel to exotic places to add pleasure to your business. The possibilities are infinite. You can only live in the present moment. Why not enjoy each and every one of them by combining business with pleasure? Bid farewell to our old friend T.G.I.F. Monday morning introduce your new motto: T.G.I.N.— Thank God It's *Now*!

competition

Competition.
When you read that word, does it make you anxious or does it make you want to flex your muscles? We all have different responses. Some people relish the opportunity to shine. They love being in the winner's circle and will go all out to get there. Others break out in a cold sweat at the thought of being the potential "loser."

When I was very young, I didn't like to compete. I think it started with birthday parties. Unlike today, when kids' parties are held at roller rinks or at Aunt Pitty-Pat's Doll House, birthday parties used to be held in backyards or basements. There were paper streamers hanging from the rafters, fruit punch, a cake, and a few games, which resulted in prizes like a jar of bubbles or packet of pick-up-sticks for the winner. This last part is where I decided I didn't want to compete.

Party games consisted of Pin the Tail on the Donkey (for which you were blindfolded and spun around in a circle until you upchucked your punch), followed by Drop the Clothespin in the Milk Bottle (if you don't know what a clothespin is and think milk always came in plastic jugs, you'll have to get an older person to explain this to you. I don't have time here.) These were boring and only slightly upsetting if you didn't win.

The real kicker was this horrible game called Musical Chairs. Chairs were placed in two rows, back to back. If there were ten kids at the party, there would be nine chairs. You see where this is going?

Uh, huh. Somebody's was going to get left out—to quote another childhood game, "The cheese would stand alone." Music would start playing, and the kids were told to march around the chairs. When the music stopped, you scrambled to find a seat. I think most of us dreaded the idea of being the only one standing—or worse, winding up on someone's lap.

I hated this game. As soon as they announced it, I felt agitated. I didn't like somebody to be left out—even if it wasn't me. The other games were a matter of skill. You took turns trying to do your best. Here, you got clobbered and smashed. Too much tension for me.

I have realized these feelings still affect me. I don't like win/lose situations all that much—unless I'm on a team. That changes the dynamic. When I'm trying to win for my teammates, as well as myself, I'm as competitive as they come.

Maybe it's because joy is best when it's shared. I was a catcher on an incredible softball team for years. We were the best in the league, season after season. These girls were some of my closest pals. To say we "went to bat" for each other is more than clever. We tried our hardest not to let the team down. When we lost, our disappointment was lessened because the cause was distributed and we didn't suffer alone. When we won, we were over the moon.

Good teamwork takes time, consistent effort, and ongoing honest communication. It takes a willingness to graciously step out of the way when a teammate is in a better position score the point. Each member of the team has to trust that the actions others take are done for the common good.

What kind of teams are you on? Do you like the spotlight or are you content to share the glory? The quality of your work life improves with the latter. Remember, winning doesn't just depend on the guy who makes the basket. It also depends on the guy who passed him the ball, and all the others who purposefully got out of his way.

That's great teamwork—and it feels good.

I suppose I really have learned a lot from my childhood. We eventually used the same milk bottle for another game called Spin the Bottle. That's one game I didn't mind playing—and really loved winning (but that's a different story).

reflections

Reflections

harvest

Harvest. I experienced one recently on a family trip to a pumpkin farm. Hundreds of parents and kids were roaming through the acres of fields on a quest for the perfect pumpkin. The farmers were seated behind huge tables laden with homemade caramel apples, jars of honey, and bags of corn for popping. People were lined up waiting to purchase these fruits of the farmers' labor.

It made me think about my family's version of the harvest. I'm not a farmer, but I do have a pretty impressive herb garden. My family and I grow the spices we use in cooking—basil, parsley, tarragon, thyme, rosemary, and mint. All summer long we water, weed, watch, and wait. Finally, the time for growing is over and our harvest begins.

Year after year, three generations of my family have been involved in cutting, cleaning, measuring, and storing the herbs. Most will be made into different sauces for pasta. Some will be frozen for use in soups and stews. The rest will season special bottles of oil and vinegar. All this makes a huge mess, and it's boring. But if we put it off, the plants will freeze and our work will have been wasted. And so, we keep working, knowing that soon we will kick back and enjoy the fruits of our labor. We anticipate the way the spicy aromas of our harvest will flood the kitchen on cold winter evenings. Meanwhile, our friends look forward to their share of our famous Passanisi Pesto. They rave about how great it is. (One can't be humble all the time).

The whole process reminds me that humans are not meant to be workhorses. We need time to rest and savor the products of our efforts: relish the feel of the clean sheets we laundered, admire the design we created, take satisfaction in the purr of the motor we just repaired, or stare in wonder at the innocent beauty of our children. These are the harvests of our lives.

Now, I know what you're thinking. Your children are nowhere near innocent and you haven't the time to sit back and gloat. But, remember, even the Creator took time to rest and appreciate His work. Are you guilty of complaining that no one notices what a great job you do, and then you don't take the time to either? I thought so. What have you harvested lately that you feel good about? Give yourself a chance to really bask in the pleasure of your accomplishments. If you don't, what's the point of working?

recess

Recess. I'm pretty sure eight out of ten young grade school kids name it as their favorite class. They just can't wait for that great little break from the daily grind of school. Don't get me wrong. You may have loved school, but without recess, all the information you spent hours trying to process was about as clear as bathwater after a mud ball fight. Fifteen minutes out of the classroom and into a quick game of dodge ball was all it took to clear up your mental fog and get your blood pumping again. You came back to math class re-energized and able to pay attention. Teachers know what they're doing when they hold recess faithfully every day. It helps kids get more out of their lessons, and more importantly, knowing that a break is coming in a short while helps kids stay focused. Imagine what school would have been like without recess. Perish the thought!

I think bosses should schedule recess like teachers do because I think it would have the same terrific impact on workers that it does on kids. It seems so obvious to me.

You sit in front of your terminal, work on the shop floor, or man your post on the sales floor for hours. If you do take a break, you probably grab a quick cup of coffee or a soda and head back. The only people outside are the smokers, and they're down on the loading dock! Does this seem like a good plan to you? I didn't think so. Where did our beloved "nap time" go?

I have a suggestion. If you are a supervisor, why don't you schedule recess for your team. A short break in the middle of the morning, and again in the afternoon. Make it a rule that no one is allowed to eat at their desk on Wednesdays and Fridays. Get a few inexpensive umbrella tables if your company doesn't have outside seating. Encourage people to go outside (tell them the office is being fumigated if you have to).

Some will actually grumble at first, especially if the weather isn't great. Tough noogies.

A shot of cold air can be invigorating and a run through the rain can feel like child's play again. You might even keep a jump rope or Nerf ball handy for the people that *really* want to relive their childhood.

If you're not the boss, schedule your own recess. Put it on your calendar so you have it to look forward to. Call a coworker you enjoy and have her join you. I see some people walking at lunch. That's good. But I'm envisioning activities that are a little more fun. Hop Scotch. Get that big fat colorful driveway chalk the preschoolers use. It washes off the blacktop. Bring your roller skates and zoom around the parking lot. No damage done. Bring bubble gum for everyone and have a bubble-blowing contest. The winner gets to pick something out of someone else's lunch. (Never underestimate the power of snacks.)

If the weather is truly nasty, get up a game of darts in the employee lounge. Write down the biggest thorn in your side at work that day on a slip of paper and tack it to the dartboard. It feels so good to stick it dead center. I was a department head in a hospital for lots of years. We used to go out and play on the kid's swings. We also had Boggle tournaments after lunch. (Boggle is a game you can buy in toy stores.) You and a coworker may keep a running chess game going for a week. I brought my stilts to work once. (My patients were very impressed.)

If you need a break FROM your coworkers, plan to do something you enjoy alone—just try to get away from your desk if possible. Go out on the lawn and practice casting with your new fishing rod. Keep a great book handy. Keep scrapbook pages in your desk and work on your photos on your break. Sit under a tree and write a letter to an old friend. It stimulates your brain, because unlike e-mail, you have to use capital letters, punctuation, and proper spelling. Send it snail mail. As often as you can, get outdoors in the fresh air and sunshine. Bundle up if you have to. You may come in red cheeked and windblown, but you'll be wide awake and ready to get back to work.

The next time the boss asks for suggestions, raise your hand and yell with all the vivacity of a ten-year-old, "Ooo, ooo, I've got a great one! How about recess?!"

reflection

Reflection. No, not the "Mirror, Mirror on the wall" kind. I'm talking about carefully thinking back, reviewing, and reconsidering your previous thoughts, words, or actions. It's a very effective continuous improvement tool that can be used in every facet of your life. Why then don't we take advantage of it? The most common arguments against reflection are, "I don't have time to think," "Why dredge up the past?" and "I can't change anything now anyway."

I feel sorry for people who think that way. They are destined to repeat the same mistakes, miss future opportunities, wallow in mediocrity, and forfeit the chance to take better control of their lives. Reflection offers an easy solution.

It doesn't require hours of solitude (although that can be wonderful), only conscious thought for the purpose of increasing your quality of life. Let's say you have a coworker who seems bent on disagreeing with you at a department meeting. Rather than allowing him to get the better of you, take a few minutes to review the encounter. Who were the other people in the room? Was he difficult with them as well? Did anyone have rapport with this guy, or was he generally negative? Was there something you did to instigate his behavior? Ask yourself how the meeting would have been if it had gone beautifully. What would have happened? What could you have done to encourage that outcome?

I'm not suggesting you assume the problem is always your fault. What I am recommending is that you take a few minutes to review, assess, and formulate a plan so that at the next meeting you can actively take a role in improving the situation. It beats dreading the next encounter or anticipating a negative interaction.

Reflection is not just for seeking out what went wrong so you can make it better. Often, quiet reflection allows us to revisit happy moments, experiencing them all over again. Think back over the day and ask yourself what was best about it. What did you enjoy most? What gave you a feeling of accomplishment? What would you like to have happen tomorrow?

This type of reflection, when followed by action, is a sure-fire method for improving performance and satisfaction in our professional and personal lives. It's the best method for breaking old habits, getting out of ruts, and keeping focus. It even gives us a chance to get to know ourselves better. It opens our eyes, hearts, and minds to endless possibilities. Not bad for something that really is "all in your head."

service

Service. Nowadays, we've confused it with "subservience." Whatever happened to the good old days of "service with a smile?" Those were the days when you pulled your car up to the pump and a uniformed fellow ran out to help you. He pumped your gas, checked under the hood, washed your windows, and even put air in your tires if they were low. Plus, he was cheerful and happy to have your business. You definitely wanted to buy gas from him again.

I miss those days. As a younger driver, I felt safer after my car had been checked out. Now, in the "Do It Yourself" era, I may wash the windows now and again, but I surely don't check the oil or the air too often—and I don't see a lot of other people doing it either. It looks like "self-serve" isn't serving us so well.

I understand the need to keep costs down, but I think we've lost sight of what service meant. We assume that if you serve, you must be a servant. This simply isn't correct. Service purely means doing something for the good of another. Isn't that the point of most of our jobs? Teachers, doctors, hairstylists, and bankers share their expertise every day. Surely, there is nothing demeaning about that.

I get the impression that a lot of people in service roles feel like second-class citizens, and it's reflected in the way they perform their duties. Wait staff who provide little or poor service, customer service reps who offer no help at all, and retail clerks who ignore customers are not uncommon. Their "this is beneath me" attitude is bad for business, and what's more, it's unhealthy for them!

As an experiment, I decided to ask people who provided me with poor service why they had done so. Were they sick? Didn't they know better? Had I done something to make them mad at me? Each time the answer was a rather sheepish, "No." I got responses like, "I'm just tired." "We don't ever have enough help around here." "I'm just working here until something better comes along." I heard that last line from a stockbroker who was selling women's shoes.

It's a shame, because these folks are in a position to provide something of value to others. If they'd only change their perspective on service, they'd find it valuable for themselves as well!

How we see our own role is our choice! Are you a servant or do you offer a professional service? These are two very different things. We can put forth our best efforts, providing quality in our product and its delivery. What you are offering isn't the issue.

One good way to improve your service is to pay attention to the service you receive, especially the best. What was exceptional? With what were you most satisfied?

Who impressed you enough that you want to do business with them again? Who made you feel taken care of or special? Review the flip-sides. What were your expectations? How did the service miss the mark? What was the attitude of the person providing the service? What could you learn from the experience?

It's so much easier to be friendly, enthusiastic, thorough, and effective when we believe that we are talented people with something of value to offer. Great service is a win/win situation!

Maybe we can't bring back our trusty gas man, but don't let "service with a smile" become a memory. Get out there and *really* serve someone—and if you want to wash my windows while you're at it, that's fine too.

reflections

Reflections

speak up!

Speak up! No, I don't mean yell. I mean voice your opinions and share your ideas. It's just amazing to me that when it comes to the workplace, so many people clam up rather than say what's on their mind or offer a suggestion.

You know what I'm talking about. The boss will hold a meeting and announce some changes that will be taking place. She asks, "Any questions? Comments?" There is minimal response. Of course, after she leaves the room, there is plenty of discussion! "Why the heck are we changing that?" "Whose big idea was this?" "Why don't they just _____?" You fill in the blank (no expletives, please).

These are questions that could have opened up valuable discussion ten minutes earlier. Now they are just grumblings and serve only to add to feelings of being ineffectual or helpless.

I see this happen all the time. Instead of telling his manager, a waiter complains to me, the customer, that the restaurant is constantly short-staffed. Flight attendants commiserate in the aisle about the decline of the airline industry while I'm buckled in my seat—a captive eavesdropper. A nurse disagrees with a doctor's decision, but rather than tell the doctor, she grumbles about it to her husband later that evening.

What good does this do? None! These people need to speak up! They have observed opportunities for improvement. They've listened to customer complaints and have ideas on how to satisfy them. Their experience, talent, and insight are being wasted! Are yours? Think about it. It serves nothing to keep your mouth shut when you can make a difference!

Most workplaces have suggestion boxes, but few employees ever use them for anything but a trash receptacle for candy wrappers. Why not make it a point to put in one of your great ideas each week? If you're not comfortable speaking in a meeting, send an e-mail to your supervisor with an idea for consideration. If you're really wussy, leave an anonymous note on his or her desk. (Hey, it's better than nothing.) If you disagree with what's going on, respectfully ask for justification of the decision and clarification of the plan. But remember, being con-frontational will get you nowhere. Instead, ask your questions in the spirit of the common good, and you will likely get the information you want. So go ahead. Make the most of those speech classes they made you take in high school. Speak up!

work

Work. It's definitely a four-letter word. Does it mean the same thing as *career*? No. In fact, there's a big difference. Want to know what it is? Try asking yourself which one you go to regularly.

Many folks define work as something they *have* to do but that they don't *want* to do. We say, "I have to work today," rather than, "I *choose* to work today."

A career is different. We choose to do it because we feel it has value. The choice factor reduces the feeling of being burdened. The perception of value tells us that our efforts have a worthwhile purpose and what we contribute is important.

So is your job work or a career? Hopefully you're not basing your feelings on a bunch of initials behind your name or the number of zeros on your paycheck. Too many people ruin their lives dwelling on letters and decimal points.

An old friend and her husband earned degrees from prestigious schools. They chose to teach in one of the poorest parts of the United States, making a grand total of about $6000 a year. When their family expanded to include three kids, they needed more income. Tim got a much better-paying job as a "garbage man." Those were his words— not "sanitation engineer" or "refuse collector." No, Tim was a "garbage man," and he loved it: the physical labor, being outdoors, discovering discarded treasure every day. While going about his regular duties, Tim looked after the people on his route. Whether that meant running the paper up to the porch in icy weather or checking that the elderly were up and about, he made being a garbage man his career. Now making $27,000 a year, he felt like a rich man. He didn't stay a garbage man forever, but at that time in his life he had chosen it—and he felt valuable.

Another friend is an orthopedic surgeon. He makes a lot of money and does a lot of good but he has little time for his family or the hobbies he used to enjoy. Though others think he has a prestigious position, it feels like a burden to him. Years ago in medical school, I'm sure he never imagined that a garbage man could be more satisfied than he.

What about your job? Remember, it's neither money nor titles that really count. The most important thing is to find joy in your work and to discover the value in it. That way, at the end of the day, you'll leave your job with something more valuable than a paycheck: satisfaction.

you

"You." It's one word repeated frequently in a pretty good comedy called *Analyze This*. It stars Robert DeNiro as a mob boss who decides he needs psychotherapy and Billy Crystal as the therapist who gets stuck treating him. Having no experience with counseling, and thus no basis of comparison, the gangster is constantly amazed at his counselor's insights and the effectiveness of his advice. Each and every time he is impressed, he points his finger at the doctor and says, "You. You. Yeah, *you*. You're good." "You" was a running gag that stayed with me because it got me thinking about "me." (I'm sure you're wondering where this is going.)

The patient in the movie was affected by the skill, approach, and unique personality of someone he had chosen to work with. I started wondering what effect I had on people who I happened to work with. Was I bringing my best to the table? Did I contribute the finer sides of my personality, or did my presence seem to suck the life out of the party?

Personality encompasses your attitudes, interests, behavioral patterns, emotional responses, and other traits that tend to stay with you for most of your life. These characteristics can be appealing or a real turnoff to others. How would others describe you? Charming, bright, upbeat, energetic, enthusiastic, wise, intriguing, deep, sexy, involved, loquacious? (Okay, I threw in that last one so you would describe me as having a great vocabulary. Look up "loquacious" later if you need to.) Think of at least ten adjectives that you feel are positive aspects of your personality. (Yes, I know there are hundreds more. You can ponder them later.) Would your list match the list your coworkers made up about you? If not, you're not sharing the best parts of yourself at work—and that's a shame because that's what makes the day so much more interesting and enjoyable for everybody.

People who don't exhibit any of their uniqueness at work are boring—and are usually bored. They tend to go through the motions like a wind-up orchestra conductor—elbows bent, arms out, arms in, arms out, arms in. No pizzazz, no passion, no flair! It's like airplane food, white cheese and white meat on white bread. Blah!

Why not let some of the more colorful sides of you out? Can you tell good stories? Do you always know a good joke? Have you got hidden talent that might be put to good use? Are you an artist, but never treat your friends to your work?

Think how much richer the workplace would be if we really let the fullness of our personalities shine through. I know a gal who has a real talent for knitting, although she never told anyone. When people commented on the beautiful sweaters she wore she'd simply say, "Oh, do you like it?" She never mentioned that she had made them. One December, she was way behind in the gifts she knitted for her family, and so she brought her knitting to work on during her lunch hour. Her teammates were astonished. They had no idea what an artist she was. When one woman begged her to teach her to knit, others chimed in with the same request. She wound up teaching a weekly class that even included several men who found knitting to be a great stress reliever as well as a creative outlet.

It's our diversity that makes us interesting, not our sameness. Can you mambo? Speak another language? Make the world's greatest pizza? Share a little more of yourself and who knows what could happen? Maybe when they're looking to give raises, fill corner offices, or honor the "employee of the year," they'll point their fingers and say, "YOU!"

you

reflections

Reflections

reflections

Reflections

spiritual

relating to the vital principle or animating force within human beings

This is perhaps the most difficult of the dimensions to comprehend. Spirit is your core, your center, your essence—that which is truly "you." This can encompass, but is not limited to, a religious belief. Ask yourself if you feel at peace. Do your beliefs give you a sense of strength? Do you feel a part of a greater whole? Or are you feeling somewhat adrift? Has your faith been shaken? Are you confused about the purpose of your life?

Have you been taking care of your spiritual life? Consider the choices you have been making. Are they working for or against you?

in this section

Altruism

Blame

Character

Consequences

Goodwill

Gratitude

Kindness

Optimism

Peace and Quiet

Pleasure

Solitude

Someday

altruism

Altruism. A big word we equate with big responsibility. "The selfless concern for the welfare of others." Our brains connect the word "altruism" to people like the late Mother Teresa and Albert Schweitzer or, more recently, Bill and Melinda Gates of Microsoft fame and fortune.

Altruists are people who have given their love, their knowledge, their time, or their financial resources. For many of them, giving comes naturally. Others may need some persuading, or "guilt tripping," as my teenage daughter, Annie, calls it. In those cases, the initial feeling of having been sucked into participating in a worthy cause is almost universally replaced by the genuine satisfaction that comes from doing good.

There are some people, however, for whom the concept of "selflessness" just doesn't click—in their heads or their hearts. Why? Are some people born to be selfish? Is being stingy with one's time and talent inherited? That's unlikely. Psychologists believe that genuine altruism requires the combination of three major ingredients.

First, an individual needs a normal brain that allows him to understand or empathize with the feelings and needs of others. Is she able to imagine herself in someone else's shoes, or lack thereof?

Second, the person must grow up in a society where compassion is valued, where learning to treat others as you want to be treated, referred to as the *Golden Rule*, is a social norm. As a child, he begins to internalize his values, moving past lip service and integrating altruism into his mind, heart, and behaviors.

Parents are the third component of the mandatory trio. They play a major role in the development of an altruist. Studies indicate that people who give selflessly had at least one parent with extremely high moral values. Altruists are from families that often discussed what was right or wrong. Even more important, they watched their role models "walk their talk."

Generosity, kindness, gentleness, inclusiveness, patience, compassion, empathy, kind-heartedness, and tolerance are virtues rarely learned from a lecture.

However, altruistic behavior is something we can learn, and it's something we can teach to others. When we do, it's good for all of us. The essence of altruism is giving with no strings attached, with no selfishness, or "What's in it for me?" But the really cool news is that the person doing the giving just may stand to benefit the most in all the dimensions of health. Talk about a gift that keeps on giving!

blame

Blame. Do you play that game? After all, it's not hard to blame something, or someone, when things go wrong. Honestly, most of us have resorted to it at one time or another. We often learn early on to fix blame outside ourselves. Ask a child, "Who spilled the milk?" and he may say, "Ernie did it." Ernie, of course, is his imaginary friend who is frequently fingered as the culprit.

As we get older, we may blame lousy teachers for our poor grades, or tons of homework for standing in the way of cleaning up our disgustingly messy rooms. Rather than outgrowing this method of explaining our shortcomings, some adults become more adept. We hear one guy blaming his lack of business success on a boss who doesn't like him; a middle-aged divorcée blaming her failed marriage on the personality defects of her ex-husband; a young mom blaming her unchecked anger on her children (whom she swears conspire to drive her crazy).

Of course, we've all felt this way occasionally. When we're tired or frustrated, it's easier to look outside ourself for excuses to justify our less-than-admirable actions. Please don't get me wrong. Thinking everything that goes wrong in the world is our fault is a whole other issue. But, blame can easily become a habit with negative consequences on all the dimensions of our health.

I wish I knew who first said, "Blaming circumstances for your behavior is like blaming the bathroom scale for your weight." That just says it all, doesn't it?

Be honest with yourself. Are you placing blame? Listen to yourself. Do you say things such as, "You make me sick," "He's driving me crazy," or "Well, if she wouldn't *something*, then I wouldn't *whatever*"? Add your own expression-traps to the list.

When we stop blaming, we can take control of our actions, our feelings, and our lives. While we must acknowledge our shortcomings, we get to take well-deserved credit for our accomplishments. It's like Mother always said, "If you want to be treated like an adult, you're going to have to act like one." So grow up a little, and leave the finger pointing to the kids!

character

Character.

That word can be interpreted in so many different ways. My father always refers to his grandkids as "real characters." He means they have lots of personality—striking individual traits that set them apart from what he considers "average." (Of course, his grandchildren would NEVER be just average!)

My daughter is involved in the theater. She is referred to by her directors as a "character" actor. That means that she is not typecast into one type of role like John Wayne, the "tough but fair guy," and Marilyn Monroe, the blonde bombshell, always were. Rather, she has the versatility to play a variety of roles involving unusual or distinctive characters. Tracey Ullman, Dustin Hoffman, and Eddie Murphy are examples that come to mind.

When it comes to your spiritual health, however, character has yet another meaning. I wish I could remember where I heard this definition of character because I've never forgotten it: *Character is the behavior you would follow if you knew you'd never be found out.* Wow! One simple sentence that says it all.

What would you do if you knew you'd never be found out? Would you cheat on an exam if you knew there'd be no chance of getting caught? Would you turn in the wallet you found that contained $500.00 in cash? Would you lie to your boss about why you were late again if he wouldn't suspect the truth? Would you pad your resume if you knew they'd never check the facts? Would you make an excuse for why you couldn't help a friend, donate money to a charity, or spend an evening with people whose company you don't enjoy?

These are not easy questions to answer. You might be thinking that diplomacy is different than lying. It's a thin line. Often we tell ourselves that we aren't telling the truth because we don't want to hurt someone's feelings. The truth is we don't like feeling uncomfortable or being put on the spot.

If you've ever seen a police show in which the suspect is subjected to a lie-detector test, you know that it's not easy to lie without having an internal reaction that the machine can detect. We may pull off fooling someone else, but we can't fool ourselves. When we lie, the balance of our well-being shifts from balanced to off-kilter. Our pulse quickens, our blood pressure increases, our temperature changes, our pattern of breathing becomes more rapid, our muscles tighten. All are easily recordable. What do you think happens to you psychologically? Fear, guilt, anxiety (to name but a few less desirable emotions).

Those who are most at ease with themselves are those whose consciences are clear. Their dispositions are strong. They consider their options and take the right actions. They make choices based on what they know in their heart to be the "right" thing to do. *Now that's character.*

Think of how all your choices add up. If your life suddenly ended will you be ready to go? Will your choices have given you peace of mind? Will you rest easy?

Today my dad is 92 years old and has Alzheimer's disease. He is no longer aware of his surroundings. But I can say unequivocally, that when he leaves this earth, he will have no enemies, no regrets, no guilt. He was a fair and good man. A character? Definitely. With character? Absolutely. I hope I honor him by following his example.

reflections

Reflections

consequences

Consequences. It's a word most of us don't like too much, probably because of everything drilled into our heads as children. "Don't touch the stove, or you'll get burned." "Clean your plate, or no dessert." "Keep frowning and your face will stick like that." (That third one rarely happened.)

Consequences didn't go away as we got older. If we didn't study in college, we failed. If we didn't show up for work, we got fired. If we didn't work at a relationship, we got dumped.

Suffering the consequences of our choices made lasting impressions. Hopefully, the pain, cost, or inconvenience we had to deal with kept us from repeating the same mistakes: painful lessons, but effective ones.

However, these days it seems we keep others, especially children, from learning those important lessons when we spare them from experiencing the consequences of their actions. When they sleep late and miss the school bus, we drive them to school. When they leave bikes in the driveway, we put them back in the garage before they're run over or stolen. When they don't eat a healthy dinner, we let them eat Goo-Goo-Pops rather than go to bed hungry.

It seems harmless at first. It's not world peace we're talking about. To you, it may seem logical and practical. After all, you don't want to have to pay for a new bicycle, deal with a child home from school on a workday, or have little Cameron go night-night with an empty tummie-wummie. (Yuck! You just can't bear the thought of him keeping you up all night with his howling.) Be honest. It's inconvenient, and dealing with it more appropriately is a pain the neck—as well as other parts of the anatomy. On deeper reflection, ask yourself what your kids have learned from their experiences. *If I leave my bike out, Mom and Dad will put it away. If it gets ruined, they'll buy me a new one. If I miss school, mom will write me a note. If I get kicked out of school, dad will get me back in. If I make a big enough fuss, I can get my way.*

As adults, we often learn too late that things can't always be fixed. We make choices all the time, and they all have consequences. Driving drunk, slacking off, and lying all have consequences. So do treating others with respect, getting an education, and taking care of the planet. The earlier we learn this rule of cause and effect, the better. *You have choices.* Before you make them, consider the consequences . . . or else.

goodwill

Goodwill. You know that word from all the Christmas carols? "Peace on earth, *goodwill* to men." It really sounds dandy in a song, but I wonder how many people really think about its meaning. It's a powerful phrase—"*Goodwill* to men."

Think about it. How much actual goodwill do you see happening around you? Not as much as we could use, I suspect. The nightly news briefs us on terrorist alerts, stock market fraud, sexual harassment, and drive-by shootings. These are definitely not examples of goodwill toward others.

On a more personal level, we experience poor service, rude salespeople, and inconsiderate drivers who seem bound and determined to kill us on the highways. It's upsetting and depressing. But it doesn't have to be this way! We can make it better. You want to know how?

First, consider your attitude. What do you think about others who share the planet? Do you consider them friend or foe? Do you look down on people who aren't as successful, gifted, or as sophisticated as you are? Pay attention to how often you use the word "them" instead of "us." This is a big clue that your perception may need a little fine-tuning.

Second, take the initiative in demonstrating goodwill (and no, this doesn't have to mean breaking the bank). Smile more, for starters. Say "please" and "thank you." Show appreciation for a job well done. Let people know when you like their product or service. Treat each of your customers as if they were your *only* customer. Take pride in the quality of your workmanship. Give the other guy a break now and then. Offer a young mother your seat on the bus. Let another driver go first. Be quiet during the movie. Recycle. Be aware of those less fortunate. Cultivate a spirit of generosity. Buy things from kids who have roadside stands. Donate your time and talent. Get involved in worthy causes like improving the environment, teaching others to read, or locating decent housing for the homeless.

Goodwill may require breaking some old habits. You may have to work on seeing things with "fresh eyes." It may require that you be a lot more aware. It definitely involves becoming more "other-centered." But it certainly won't kill you, and I guarantee it will be well worth the effort.

And what will come of all this goodwill? Who knows . . . maybe that "peace on earth" we're always singing about.

gratitude

Gratitude. As children, we were taught to say "thank you" a lot—and most of us still do. But did you ever think about how often we use those two words but never really experience the "feeling" that should accompany them—gratefulness or appreciation for something that's been done for or given to us.

Without thinking, we say "thanks" to the grocery store bagger, the FedEx guy, the telephone information lady, the dental hygienist, the fast food drive-up window kid, and the gray-haired Wal-Mart greeter. It's a matter of habit. But it's rare that we really stop and feel grateful for the bagger who lugged our bags to the car in pouring rain, for the FedEx guy who always remembers our dog's name and brings him a treat, for the hygienist who worked into her lunch break to get us out in time for a meeting, for the correct order handled by the fast food server, and for the consistently good-natured humor of the Wal-Mart greeter.

Today, prayer is a common outlet for gratitude. We say we're giving thanks for all our blessings—our health, our family, our job, and opportunities. I think many times the words are rote. Take a minute to really think about what you're grateful for and experience the wonderful feelings that arise. If we reframe our thinking a little bit, the things we gripe about can become things to be truly thankful for. "Wow. I woke up this morning. Considering the alternative, that's definitely good." "Thanks for the functioning kidneys that wake me up in the middle of the night." "Thanks for the perfect hearing that allows me to hear my

teenager try to sneak in
an hour after curfew,
and the fact that he's
alive." "Thanks for a
job that gives me the
opportunity to work
forty-five hours a week
and make a little overtime
pay." "Thanks that I have a
mother who loves me enough
to meddle." "Thanks for my
husband's snoring—it assures me
that he is alive."

You see, not all blessings involve
winning the lottery, losing thirty pounds,
or retiring at the age of fifty. If you're only
grateful for the big stuff, you miss out on all
those good feelings you could be having. Think about those blessings
in disguise, and you'll have endless chances to really feel gratitude—
and that something to be grateful for!

Kindness

Kindness. Why is something so nice becoming extinct? I don't think this is a recent phenomenon. No, I'm pretty sure it's been creeping up gradually, like an old pair of undies with stretched-out elastic—not uncomfortable at first, but all of a sudden, a sticky problem that needs attention.

Back when I was a younger mother, I started noticing things: drivers making rude hand signals, a general absence of "please" and "thank you," and a lack of awareness or concern that we share the planet with others. Have you noticed litter-lined roadways, people barging through life in their own little worlds, and how often one shopper lets a door slam shut in the face another? Come on, people!

This all came to a head on a day I was driving kiddie-carpool. I was stopped at a light with five 4-year-olds harnessed into their seats. For fifteen miles I had listened to their usual style of conversation. Every other comment was "What's that?" or "Why?" Since they were all learning to read, their attention was drawn to the bumper sticker on the pickup truck in front of us. It wasn't one of those braggy ones announcing, "My Child is an Honor Student at Myrtles College of Electrolysis," or a political one like, "Nuke the Whales." This was one of the nasty ones. You've seen the type—"Don't Like My Driving? Call 1-800-EAT- S _ _ _!"

There I sat, listening to these kids sounding out the word. Trying to distract them, I'd point out the back window. "Is that an alien spacecraft?" "Look, free ponies!" My diversionary tactics were futile. They all figured out the dirty word at the same time and I knew it was one they would repeat. Their horrified parents would interrogate them: "Where did you learn that bad word?" They would answer honestly, "In Mrs. Passanisi's car." Oh, great.

This type of rudeness and lack of civility surround us all too often. During prime time, we hear TV families calling each other awful names, saying hateful things. This is supposed to be funny?

It's time we put down our collective Nike-clad feet and turn this trend around! It isn't healthy for us as individuals, nor as a society. In the long run, rudeness lessens us as human beings and adversely affects our mental and social health.

Honestly, can't we go back to being kind, to showing a little respect for one another? Growing up, we were all told to "be nice" about fifty million times. I say it's high time we wake up and do it!

optimism

Optimism.

I started thinking about it when I took a crash course for computer illiterates. The instructor asked me if my computer had "WYSIWYG (pronounced WIZ-ee-wig) capability." Say what?! He explained the term is an acronym for "What you see is what you get." I got a mental picture of the late Flip Wilson's crazy character Geraldine saying those exact words.

I've found that when it comes to optimism, WYSIWYG applies to life in general. We tend to get what we see, or what we expect. (Why else would books on visualization be so popular?)

Optimism is defined as "an inclination to anticipate the best possible outcome." Psychologists tell us that optimists seek out, remember, and expect pleasurable experiences. It's an active priority for them.

All optimists expect good things to happen—but for different reasons. Some credit their talent; some think they're just lucky; others attribute their good fortune to their faith in God, Buddha, Allah, or another higher power. Whatever the reason, the optimist tends to fill her mind with positive thoughts and visions of desirable outcomes. She *expects* to be pleased. Because of this pattern of thinking and behavior, negative ideas are crowded out. The marvelous side effect is that an optimistic outlook seems to have a very positive impact on health.

Researchers have been investigating the role of optimism on immune function and longevity, and the results are *optimistic*, as expected. The important thing to remember is this: How we see things is always a choice. Like any other habit, our perspectives become ingrained.

Think of someone you know whom you consider to be an optimist. Then think of someone else you think is a pessimist. What are the differences between them? Pay close attention to how they explain why something has turned out a certain way. If the optimist receives poor service from a salesperson, she may believe it's because the store is understaffed and the staff is overworked. She doesn't feel that she's been singled out for being mistreated. On the other hand, when the pessimist gets the same bad service, he is more likely to feel that he was intentionally neglected because of his age, race, manner of dress, etc. He takes it personally. His experience colors further shopping experiences. He now tends to expect bad service. You often hear him commenting, "Nobody cares anymore. You just can't get good service." He has a chip on his shoulder and you'd better believe it affects his whole life. He expects the worst, and he gets it!

The choice is yours. Do you want to be an optimist or a pessimist? Before you choose, remember, "What you see is what you get" (or WYSIWYG for you computer nerds out there).

peace and quiet

Peace and quiet. We all know how great it is for us, and yet it's hard to come by. We may beg our kids for a little peace and quiet. Our doctor may prescribe a few weeks of peace and quiet. We all want and need it occasionally. Yeah, right. How often does that happen?

Take the second part first. Quiet—a precious commodity these days. We are constantly bombarded by noise. Outside it's traffic, sirens, jackhammers, and jumbo jets. Inside it's even worse. Workers are subjected to ear-piercing heavy machinery or the constant drone of copy machines, computer printers, telephones, elevator Muzak, and coworker phone conversations.

We look forward to relaxing at home. But the first thing many of us do is flip on the TV or stereo, adding to sounds of the phone, doorbell, microwave, washing machine, garbage disposal, blow dryer, and video games—not to mention kids and pets.

Because human beings are amazingly adaptable, we often become less conscious of certain everyday sounds.

But all that noise can have negative effects—high blood pressure, muscular tension, irritability, nervousness, and significant loss of hearing are but a few. Constant exposure to noise affects our relationships, too. We start tuning out more and really listening less. Noise even affects the crime rate and number of suicides. The worse the noise, the higher the numbers.

We get so accustomed to noise that silence can be awkward or unnerving. It shouldn't be! Quiet is a time of healing and rejuvenation. It's where we can find some peace—peace that comes through reduced external stimulation, quiet reflection, simple awareness, or prayer. Quiet is the cause, peace is the effect.

So, the next time your body needs to unwind, your brain needs to calm down, and your spirit needs attention, turn off the TV and seek out some quiet. That, my friends, is the precursor to inner peace.

pleasure

Pleasure. Where did all this guilt come from? Why has "pleasure" become a dirty word? Hello! Enjoyment is a good thing—plain and simple.

I don't know where we got the idea that what's good for us has to be boring, distasteful, or difficult. But we ought to clear it up right now. Think about it. The desire for pleasure evolved to increase our chances for survival. Tasty food leads us to eat, love encourages us to reproduce. Taking care of the earth or others gives us a feeling of satisfaction. You see—much of what feels good and right to us is beneficial for our health and is necessary for the survival of the human race.

Many of the good things available in life—friends, family, good food, making love—are pleasurable. Often our instincts can point us in the right direction. Think about some of the things you enjoy: a Sunday afternoon nap, a hot shower, a soothing massage, your kitty curled up on your lap, the serenity you experience while fishing. The good feelings we get tell us we are on the right track.

I know some of you are skeptical. You believe in the "no pain, no gain" philosophy of health. You lead a Spartan existence, believing your sacrifices will pay off in good health and long life. Well, they certainly will make your life *seem* a lot longer. Actually, it may not make as big a difference as you think, unless you have serious medical problems that warrant such strict guidelines. Rather, we're learning that many of life's pleasures have health benefits—loving relationships, beautiful scenery, music, long walks in the woods, a good book, and even long hours at work (provided we enjoy them).

Granted, too much of some good things may not be in our best interest. The rule of thumb is usually moderation. But in some cases, more really is better. Some of life's greatest blessings fall into that category. Add as many of those to your day as you can. It's time to stop feeling guilty about seeking pleasure. The simple, delightful beauties of life are nothing your mother would be ashamed of! So, go ahead! Enjoy!

solitude

Solitude.

Frankly, it sounds pretty good at this point. I had a good week that was spent working with hundreds of people. I enjoyed them all. Now I just want to be alone.

Sadly, this isn't always easy—especially at home. There are often children, pets, significant others, parents, neighbors, etc., to keep me from being alone. They often get their feelings hurt if we politely suggest they go elsewhere (or get even more upset if we aren't so polite). I know that wanting to be alone instead of with others may sound hard-hearted, but it's something we all need for our health, not to mention our sanity. It's no reflection on our feelings for others. In fact, our being alone often benefits others because it keeps us from losing our temper with them or screaming at them like banshees.

Life and health are based on balance. We exercise—we sleep. We laugh—we cry. We need other people—and we need to be alone.

The time we spend alone can be used in an infinite number of ways. We can "veg out" and do nothing. We can daydream or think about our life goals. We can ponder the universe or envision our future. These things need solitude so we can really get in touch with our feelings, our values, and the things that matter most to us.

Being alone is great for us because it gives us a time to be "off duty"— time when we don't have to answer to anyone, talk, or compromise.

We can just be with ourselves and do whatever feels "just right" to us at that moment in time.

Some people find being alone is uncomfortable. It makes them restless, nervous, or bored. Okay, it might take a little getting used to. But, solitude can be a welcome relief and a time of healing.

Solitude is a valuable gift we can give each other out of love and understanding—and it costs nothing. The next time you find yourself alone, relish those moments. Heaven knows they may be few and far between. So, whenever and wherever you can, grab them. Just be with yourself and your thoughts. These moments can get you in touch with your deepest self. So, make time for solitude now. That way you won't find yourself screaming at the people you love: "Leave me alone!"

someday

Someday. It's become the eighth day of the week—Sunday, Monday, Tuesday, Wednesday, Thursday, Friday, Saturday, *Someday*. *Someday*, I'm going to travel. *Someday*, I'll quit this job and open a doll shop. *Someday*, I'm going to lose twenty pounds. *Someday*, I'll go back to school. *Someday*, I'll spend more time with my family. Have you noticed how many people are trying to live in *someday* instead of in the present?

I hear that word so often that I wonder what percentage of people ever get around to doing the things they've postponed until *someday*. I'll bet it's a small percentage. And it's too bad, because fate often intervenes or time simply runs out.

I knew a very hard-working woman. She and her husband always talked about moving to a cabin in the mountains of Kentucky. "Someday," they said. They waited until they were close to 70 years of age. Sadly, the husband died of a heart attack while they were moving their furniture into their cabin. Their dream was never realized.

We should think very carefully about what experiences we want our life's journey to include and when we want them to happen. Make a list of the things you would like to do, have, or be. Review it and decide which ones can happen sooner rather than later. Sure, it's fine to save some money for a rainy day, but enjoy a little treat or luxury now and then—maybe box seats to a great game or buying a piece of art that feeds your soul. It's fine to schedule the big family reunion for next summer—but go ahead and invite the grandkids over this weekend. If you've always wanted to travel, get something on the calendar now. You can only live in the present. Actually, enjoying your life today may actually help you stay healthy enough to do the rest of the things you've put off for SOMEDAY. Just don't wait too long! After all, visiting the Grand Canyon is a whole lot more awesome when you still have your eyesight!

reflections

Reflections

reflections

Reflections

Special Thanks

I'd like to thank everyone who helped me with this book—but no one did. Just kidding! I can't honestly say it was a labor of love, but I can say it was labor—helped enormously by so many. The following terrific people have my gratitude. Each is a blessing in my life for which I am eternally grateful.

Peter Passanisi, husband and creative partner extraordinaire, who got the idea for this book in the first place and pushed me relentlessly to "get it down and get it done." There would be no book without Pete. His faith in my talent is overblown and definitely biased.

Annie Passanisi, my quirky, artsy, college student daughter and the real writer in the family. As content editor she made this book so much better by creatively combining her words with my own. A typical kid, she has already thrown most of my advice back in my face.

My parents, Friedrich and MaryAnne Keller, who gave me a happy childhood and a good education that provided a springboard to whatever I wanted to do.

Mary Janet Ruff, a former middle school principal, and my longtime friend, now my right arm/left brain overqualified office administrator and way-too-much-fun travel pal. Without her, little gets done, including my hair. My work life is so much more fun with her in it. She is truly a multi-purpose pal who never stops going the extra mile.

Ed Murray, who put me on the radio and challenged me to present material that was solid, positive, and easy to hear. Working for him was like having four term papers due a week, but I loved our Sunday morning radio conversations.

Bobbi Linkemer, experienced author and friend, who expertly guided me through the process of putting a book together.

Steven Michels-Boyce, a gifted artist, whose vision and gift adds color and life to my words. I look forward to the future, working with such a unique and special talent.

Michael McConnell, my totally tuned-in copy editor, whose expertise and open mind corrected and improved my work while keeping it "mine."

Trese Gloriod, who designed the layout and interior design of the book. Her young, fresh eyes made my words look interesting, profound and organized—all at the same time.

Sam Horn, accomplished author and advisor, for her creative input and reassurance that my words have value, especially through stories.

My writing buddies, author Fawn Germer and Pam Vaccaro (also known as The Peep Sisters), who helped me find my "voice" and made me write when I wanted to play hookey. Our hot tub conversations convinced me I could actually pull this off. I relish our creative time together.

My Master Mind buddies, Lois Creamer, Pam Vaccaro, and Nancy Wegge, who offer me emotional support, honest opinions, and wise counsel whenever I need it, which is often. I can't wait to bring this final product for "show and tell."

From the Fischer Ross Group, Grada Fischer, who believed in my speaking talent and told me years ago that if I captured my words and thoughts in a book, it would be easier to market me. (So, can you get me on Oprah now?) And to Lee Houck for his gentle, yet honest critiques. His writing will be much more famous than mine one day.

Skip and Nancy Herndon, my extraordinarily generous friends, who offered their beautiful Arizona home as a writer's retreat more than once. They asked only that I "pay it forward." I swear I didn't screw up the pool filter but I'm sorry I drained the hot tub.

My other dear close pals, Debbie Sigrist, my grade school hypochon-driac best friend who helped me through my mother's passing as an empathetic hospice nurse. And Karyn Buxman, soul sister and healer/speaker pro. It's amazing what diet Snackwells and red wine can do for a friendship.

My former patients, their families, and all the health care team members with whom I worked over all these years. I am honored to have walked the path with you during challenging and interesting times.

I am blessed to have connected with so many of you in my practice, my life, and my audiences over the years. You have shared your stories, your challenges, your pain, and your triumphs—the real deal, no holds barred. I am awed by your honesty and contributions for the benefit of others.

I have so many other great pals and people of influence who con-tribute to every facet of my well-being. They all know who they are, and I'm sure they're big enough not to mind not being mentioned here by name.

And to all of you who have encouraged me to write, assuring me that if I did, you would buy my books. I took names. So, when can I expect your order?

We'd love to hear from you!!

To order additional copies of IT'S YOUR LIFE—CHOOSE WELL and other works by Kathleen Passanisi contact:

MOVERE PUBLISHING

1-866-MOVERE1

MOVERE
PUBLISHING

Ask about quantity discounts and signings.

Are you interested in having Kathleen Passanisi speak to your group?

Do you want to learn more about her presentations and products?

Would you like to send her an e-mail?

Check out   **www.kathleenpassanisi.com**

hear from you!

Steven Michels-Boyce

Cover Design and Illustration

phone: 612-822-8545

e-mail: emby@visi.com

Trese Gloriod

Graphic Design and Illustration
idsign@usa.net
314·428·4283

about the author

About the Author

Recipient of the 2003 Lifetime Achievement Award from The Association for Applied and Therapeutic Humor, Kathleen Keller Passanisi is best known for her hysterical sense of humor, her solid background in health care, and for sixteen years (and counting) of bringing down the house as a professional speaker.

Her expertise in wellness and therapeutic humor has made her one of the most popular presenters on quality of life issues today. Whether it's a thousand women, a hundred rocket scientists, or twenty cancer patients, Kathleen has them rolling in the aisles and learning at the same time.

After decades in health care, several years serving as the "wellness" advisor on a St. Louis radio show, and speaking to hundreds of thousands of people in her audiences, she has finally done what her patients and fans have asked her to do for years—write a book. (She is also a contributing author of HUMOR ME: America's Funniest Humorists on the Power of Laughter.)

She is delighted that you have a copy of her book, since her biggest fear is seeing her hard work sitting on the "Bargain Books" table at the flea market.

When she's not flying around the country speaking, Kathleen lives in Lake Saint Louis, Missouri (until she has enough money to retire to the beach), with her husband, Peter, their daughter, Annie, and their dog, Kramer.